HOW TO
SPECIALIZE
IN
STAMP COLLECTING

HOW TO
SPECIALIZE
IN
STAMP COLLECTING

Bill Olcheski

David McKay Company, Inc.
New York

**For Rosemary
who always
makes life
worth the
effort**

Copyright © 1981 by Bill Olcheski

Library of Congress Cataloging in Publication Data

Olcheski, Bill.
How to specialize in stamp collecting.
Includes index.
1. Postage-stamps—Collectors and collecting—
Handbooks, manuals, etc.   I. Title.
HE6215.O474   769.56′075   81-80362
ISBN 0-679-20681-7   AACR2

Book Design: ARLENE SCHLEIFER GOLDBERG

1 2 3 4 5 6 7 8 9 10

Manufactured in the United States of America

7034083

Contents

Acknowledgments

I am indebted to many people for assistance in gathering the material for this book, especially the members of the Edward Douglass White Stamp Club of Arlington, Virginia, who took the time to discuss their hobby with me at great length. I will not attempt to identify individual members who helped, since to do so invites the danger of skipping the names of some who deserved to be recognized. All have my gratitude.

I must give special recognition to Mr. Bill Waugh, my stamp buddy for many years. He is a great source of technical knowledge; some of the illustrations are borrowed from his collection.

Introduction

Once you have mastered the basics of stamp collecting, you are ready to diversify. This is an interesting and often a necessary step. Interesting because it allows you to move into areas that are of special interest to you—necessary because it is often frustrating to try to keep up with the eight thousand or so new issues that are released each year around the world.

This book is designed to help you bridge the gap between general collecting and the many areas of specialization open to you. It does not attempt to give you detailed information about any particular kind of collecting. Rather, it is a kind of "sampler" designed to pique your appetite for more information. That's when you will want to contact one or more of the specialized societies and publications that will be happy to provide you with additional information about their groups and their approaches to the hobby. You will find dozens of them listed in the Directory of Specialized Groups, Chapter 16 of this book.

If you haven't joined a stamp society or club by now, you should seriously consider doing so. Solo collecting can be fun, but you miss the pleasure of swapping stamps and stamp stories with other collectors.

Choosing the right stamp dealer also becomes important at this point in your collecting life. This book devotes a chapter to telling you points to check in picking a dealer with whom you may be doing business for many years. This dealer will become more than a source of stamps and supplies. He or she can be a valuable source of the technical information you will need periodically.

You will also be introduced to the world of stamp auctions, one of the sources of stamps you will want to explore. The chapter on auctions tells you where to find them and how to make successful bids. It also shows you how to prepare material you might want to enter into an auction.

The chapter on stamp shows tells you how to add enjoyment and cut the cost of attending a stamp show. It also outlines the steps to follow in organizing a stamp show in your local club.

The chapter called "Just for Fun" gives you some philatelic trivia quizzes you might want to work alone or share with collectors in your club.

You will be introduced to "treasure hunting," which gives tips on the tools you will need and the kinds of items for which you will be looking.

There are chapters on topical collecting, block collecting, postal card collecting, and the fascinating world of revenues and tax stamps found on the back pages of your album.

The collecting of United Nations issues is a hobby by itself, and one chapter is devoted to UN stamps and other philatelic items.

Another chapter talks about buying and selling collections. It takes you behind the scenes and shows you what a dealer looks for in appraising a collection—including a detailed description of a system you will want to use if you contemplate buying a collection from another collector.

Read on. Dig in and discover that the fun you had when you began collecting was just a start, and that the best is yet to come!

Happy collecting.

1

A Touch of History

Stamp collecting is not a very old hobby. The introduction of the postage stamp goes back only to 1840, when the famous one-penny black of Great Britain was placed on sale.

Rowland Hill, in his work *Post Office Reform: Its Importance and Practicality*, suggested a basic inland letter rate for Great Britain regardless of the distance, an idea that caught the imagination of both the press and business in 1839.

His uniform penny postage made it possible for the sender to drop his letter into convenient letter boxes; a letter carrier would deliver the mail as fast as he could walk. Under the earlier system most letters were mailed unpaid and the postmen had to waste time finding an address, calculating the charges to be levied, and waiting at each address for the necessary payment.

The penny rate remained in force from 1840 until 1918, the only revision during the three quarters of a century being in the weight allowed.

The postage stamp itself was a byproduct of the Uniform Penny Postage Act, and a competition to determine the method by which prepayment of postage was to be effected was promoted by the United Kingdom Treasury. It eventually was Rowland Hill himself who created the simple design that became the world's first postage stamp.

When the Universal Postal Union was founded in 1874, all member countries were required to inscribe their names on their postage stamps. The United Kingdom, in deference to its role as the pioneer of adhesive postage stamps, was exempt from the requirement. Instead, the head of the reigning monarch was considered sufficient identification. To this day, Great Britain is the only nation in the world that does not have its name on its postage stamps.

Hill received many honors for his postal work. He was knighted, given a parliamentary grant and a lifetime pension. When he died in 1879, he was buried in Westminster Abbey, an honor reserved for monarchs and Britain's most famous men.

On August 22, 1979, the postal service of Great Britain issued a set of four commemorative stamps to mark the centennial of the death of Rowland Hill. The four stamps also appeared on a miniature sheet. The souvenir sheets carried a surcharge to help finance the 1980 International Stamp Exhibition scheduled in London.

GREAT BRITAIN was one of many countries paying postal tribute to Sir Rowland Hill in 1979. The British issued this set of four stamps.

A portrait of Rowland Hill was shown on the 10p stamp; a bellman—an early nineteenth-century postman—appeared on the 11½p value. The 13p featured the London post of 1801–1840 with a postman of the time; and the 15p depicted a Victorian lady and her child posting a letter.

Rowland Hill commemoratives have also been issued by many other countries

2

Treasure Hunting

The dream of finding a stamp "treasure" is in the back of the mind of every collector. One of the first stories most stamp collectors learn is about the fabulous find of William T. Robey.

He was the man who in 1918 purchased a sheet of the twenty-four-cent airmail at the post office and discovered that, on the pane that he had bought, the airplane was inverted. Within a week he had sold it for $15,000, a real fortune in those days. The pane has been broken up and sold many times since then. Current value of a block of four—many thousands of dollars—is always quoted when new stamp catalogs are released each year.

Few of us will be fortunate enough to find a prize of this magnitude, but postal errors—particularly on issues of the United States—continue to bring rewards far beyond their face value.

As the United States moved into producing multicolored stamps, often requiring several runs through the press, the possibility of error multiplied; there are hundreds of variations in color and perforation shifts. There are so many, in fact, that some auction houses specialize in the handling of such varieties.

If I might be permitted a personal note, I will share with you a story about a discovery of my own. I was doing a mailing to promote my stamp newsletter and had decided that—since the newsletter was aimed at collector families—we could probably find subscribers among members of a Catholic group. The necessary mailing pieces were prepared and my daughter was dispatched to the post office to pick up the necessary postage. She returned with 100 panes of the family-planning stamp. I was explaining to her the impracticality of using a stamp on this subject for mailing to that group when I noticed that one of the panes appeared unusual. It had an obvious perforation shift. The plate number was inside the first row of stamps and the denomination was shifted completely off the first row of stamps. It was on the wrong side on the rest of the stamps.

I have kept the pane as a conversation piece although it is now worth several hundred dollars as a pane and would be worth more if broken up and sold as singles or blocks.

The keys to treasure hunting are knowledge of stamp values (which you can gain by studying the catalogs) and an eye for the unusual, which will come to you as you handle more and more stamps.

Take a perforation gauge with you when you treasure-hunt. A difference in perforations can often mean a big difference in value between stamps that look alike.

Perforations are measured by sliding the stamp up and down the scale of the perforation gauge until the black dots on the gauge fit exactly into the holes at the edges of the stamp. Perforations are always measured across the top and down the sides of the stamp.

Among recent U.S. issues, the nine- and thirteen-cent stamps issued in 1977 in booklet form are worth many times more when perforated 10 x 10 than when perforated 11 x 10½.

The common red two-cent Washington stamps of the designs issued in the 1920s come with several different perforations. A copy perforated 11 x 10 catalogs about thirty dollars, while the commonest ones, perforated 12 or 11 x 10½, can still be purchased for a few cents per hundred.

There are valuable perforation varieties among foreign stamps as well. The author once found a couple of copies of Grenada's two-and-one-half-pence King George VI stamps perforated 12½ x 13½ in an envelope in which most other copies of the same stamp were perforated 12½ on all four sides. Those perforated 12½ x 13½ now catalog about one hundred dollars each used, while the other varieties catalog only fifteen cents.

Another factor which can make a big difference is the watermark. Whether a stamp is watermarked or not, and which mark is used, can be major value determinants.

The one-dollar purple-and-black Wilson stamp of the U.S. Presidential Series of 1938 was normally issued on unwatermarked paper and in that variety catalogs about fifteen cents in used condition.

However, in 1951, a small quantity was printed by accident on watermarked paper designed for use on revenue stamps. Those one-dollar Wilson stamps with the watermark catalog twenty-five dollars each, cancelled. The watermark is usually visible to the naked eye if the stamp is held up to the light.

Train your philatelic eye to spot stamps that appear unusual. In 1909, some of the regular issue of U.S. stamps and some of the two-cent Lincoln commemorative of that year were printed on an experimental paper that is described in the catalog as "bluish." This is really a poor description, as the paper is more of a gray than a blue shade. The color is visible on both the front and back of the stamp.

Discovering one of the "bluish paper" stamps is a real find. The common one-center of that period on white paper is in the nickel catalog range. The same stamp on the so-called "bluish paper" catalogs fifty dollars.

Be careful. If the stamp is really blue, you have a phony — a home-made job some con artist tried to create by using diluted ink.

Grills were used on U.S. stamps from 1867 to the early 1870s. They consisted of indentations placed in the stamp to break the paper fibers and cause the ink to spread when the cancellation was applied. The goal was to prevent reuse of the stamps by washing or otherwise removing the cancellation. The grilled stamps of 1867 came with grills of various sizes, some of them very rare and all of them worth more than the stamps of the same design previously issued without the grill.

The 1869 U.S. issue normally comes with a grill. The so-called "bank note" issues of 1870-89 were first issued with grills in 1870. Grilling was discontinued a few months later. These "bank note" issues with the grill are worth the hunt.

The earlier grills are easy to recognize. But some of the 1870 – 71 grills are hard to spot, being grilled very lightly with only a few points of the grill showing.

As mentioned, the purpose of the grills was to prevent reuse of the stamps. In another crime-prevention effort, the United States created the Kansas-Nebraska overprints of 1929.

The plan was to overprint the stamps of the 1926 – 27 series with the name of the states and then — if a batch of stamps from Kansas turned up in New York or California—the authorities would become suspicious and investigate for possible theft. The scheme obviously did not work. It was tried in two states and then abandoned. The Kansas-Nebraska set consists of eleven stamps overprinted from each state, ranging in face value from one cent through ten cents. They are not attractive stamps. They were printed on rotary presses and the centering is poor.

The uniqueness of the idea and the fact that it was abandoned after a short period have caused the stamps to rise in value each year. This has led to the appearance of many counterfeits, some of them crudely done on a typewriter. The fakes are easier to spot, particularly on mint stamps, since the overprint was applied before the gum and anything put on afterwards makes an indentation in the gum.

Not all "treasure" finds are spectacular. But, knowledgeable collectors can come up with "finds" at almost any stamp show just by rummaging through the boxes of stamps dealers have priced at a few cents apiece. These boxes often are the result of a dealer simply not having time to go through a large lot; they are tossed into the box just to get them out of the way.

The first thing to look for is stamps that catalog considerably more than the asking price. This is where your knowledge of prices—acquired through catalog research—pays off. It may enable you to spot a stamp the dealer has overlooked in his pricing.

Next, look for stamps that fit specialized parts of your collection. These could be various topicals, stamps of certain countries, precancels, perforated initials, and so on down the list. You may not find a rarity, but you will fill some album spaces at low cost.

U.S. COVER showing advertising corner card of a small-town hotel plus a railway mail cancellation.

Keep an eye out for anything else that looks interesting. Unusual cancellations fit this category: bullseye (on the nose) cancels, numerical cancellations of many countries, pictorial cancellations, special markings that indicate the stamp has been carried on railway or highway post offices or processed at a railroad station in some foreign country. All of these categories have their own following and it should be easy to find someone to trade your discovery with even if it doesn't fit into your personal collection. As a general rule, any stamp that looks unusual or different is worth the few-cents' gamble just to get it home and check it out.

DUTCH NUMBER CANCEL. In the 19th century each Dutch post office had a number, which it used in its cancel.

PRETTY "BULLSEYE" cancel from Finland.

FRENCH "CONVOYEUR" cancel, indicating railway service on secondary lines. The outside wavy oval is characteristic of cancels of this type.

Before you begin working on a bunch of unsorted U.S. stamps, assemble your philatelic tool box. You will need a stamp catalog, a good magnifying glass, a perforation gauge, and a watermark detector. As you get more involved in treasure hunting, you may want to add an ultraviolet light for detecting "phosphor-tagged" stamps, and a few color charts to aid in separating various stamp shades.

Look to your stamp catalogs for help in separating the early U.S. issues. Scott provides a very helpful stamp identifier in its U.S. specialized catalog. This section should be "must reading" for anyone who wants to seriously tackle the job of separating the early U.S. issues. On the two-cent Washington issue of 1903, for instance, specialists recognize several different shades of red-type colors. There also were two different dies used in the various printings, and the catalog clearly illustrates the heavier lines of the Number II die. This is not an expensive stamp, but some varieties catalog as much as five times the value of other types of the same stamp.

Perhaps the most confusing issues of U.S. stamps occurs in the definitive issues of 1908–1909 and 1908–21. Portraits of Franklin appear on the one-centers and of George Washington on the two-cent stamps.

The easiest initial sorting is to separate the stamps that have the value spelled out instead of being shown in numbers. These are the stamps of the earlier issue. After that, the sorting process gets more complicated.

There are flatbed and rotary-press printings, watermarked and unwatermarked varieties, and shading and perforation differences.

The differences in the various types are clearly illustrated in the specialized catalog, with description of areas in which the shading, for instance, is heavier in one type of stamp than in others.

Our purpose here is not to go into extensive detail on the myriad of differences, since they would fill a book by themselves. Rather, the intent is to make you aware that the differences exist, that they sometimes turn up in unsorted mixes, and that they can make a substantial difference in the value of a stamp. Your stamp dealer can point you to more in-depth coverage of any of the specialized types of screening described in this chapter.

Treasure hunting doesn't end with stamps. Knowledgeable collectors can make good "finds" in cover boxes as well.

Postal stationery is growing in popularity and there are many postal cards, aerogrammes, letter sheets, and just plain commercial covers to be found in cover boxes.

A collector who is lucky enough to find a box of old love letters in an attic can have a field day with the envelopes—not to mention the romantic prose they contain. The stamps may be of minimal value since they probably represent the common first-class rate of the period, but the envelopes could be a different story. If you find such an accumulation, don't make the mistake of cutting the stamps off the envelopes, as this could greatly reduce the value of the cover to which they were attached.

Look at the dates, remembering that early first-day

THIS SIDE OF CARD FOR ADDRESS

Mr. Charles C. Colman

1836 Euclid Avenue

Cleveland 15, Ohio

REPLY POSTAL CARD

United States of America

THIS SIDE IS FOR ADDRESS ONLY

RALPH W. DUNBAR,

23 COURT STREET.

BOSTON.

TREASURE HUNTS in cover boxes can yield interesting postal cards. This selection includes a flag cancel, an early-reply card, a revalued card, and two old penny-postal cards.

covers were not identified as such. Your catalog will tell you the issue date and you can match it against the date on your cover. If the dates coincide, you could have a real find.

Interesting cancellations abound on U.S. covers and postcards. They provide a wealth of material for collectors of flag cancels and early machine cancellations. Other interesting variations include railway cancels, ship cancels, and cancellations from military post offices.

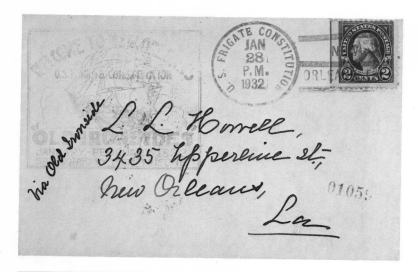

NAVAL COVER *from U.S.S.* Constitution.

APO COVER, *typical of those used by military post offices overseas. "APO" stands for Army Post Office. Navy covers of the same type carry the letters "FPO," for Fleet Post Office.*

The cover boxes also may yield unusual advertising covers, covers used at exhibitions, and other variations. A quick review of the chapter on postal cards will alert you to varieties to watch for in cover boxes.

Picture postcards often turn up in boxes of this type. Collecting them for their pictures is a widespread hobby, but the philatelist is more interested in their stamps and cancellations.

3

Topical Collecting

Perhaps the easiest kind of stamp collecting to get into—and hence one of the most popular—is the collecting of topicals. As the name implies, this involves the collecting of stamps that feature a particular subject, theme, or topic. What this can include is limited only by your imagination. It can be a broad category such as outer space, animals, or flowers, or it can be more limited to such specialties as chess, synagogues, and the like.

The biggest appeal in topical collecting is that it requires no special knowledge of philately beyond knowing how to mount a stamp in an album and how to use a stamp catalog.

Topical collectors as a rule are not concerned by the fact that there may be several varieties of a single stamp—coil, booklet pane, sheet stamp, watermarked or unwatermarked, or even perforation differences. The mere fact that a stamp shows the subject or theme being collected is considered sufficient reason to add it to the collection.

Topical collectors are not particularly concerned with the country from which the stamp comes, or with the value of the individual stamp.

The stamps collected can be mounted in specialized albums prepared for them. Many collectors, however, prefer to mount the stamps on blank pages and then add appropriate decorations of their own.

There are several disadvantages to this type of collecting. The first is that the wide variety of ways in which collectors choose to display such stamps makes it difficult to keep track of what they have. If the stamps are mounted without regard to country or catalog number, it is virtually impossible to determine which stamps are needed and which you already have. Further, if you decide to switch from a topical to a general collection, it creates the need to go back and catalog each stamp, remove it from the topical collection, and then remount it in a more suitable album. This also poses problems when a collection is sold, unless it is sold to another topical collector, since the buyer has little basis on which to determine a fair price.

The obvious answer is to introduce some system into your collecting regardless of the topic you choose to follow. It takes just a moment to pencil in a catalog number under a stamp. This makes it much easier when you want to make an inventory or a want list. It also gives you the basis for an insurance claim if the collection is lost, stolen, or destroyed.

Once you select a topic or theme, look around to see what checklists are available of the stamps that reasonably belong in your collection. For the broader categories like space on stamps, there are printed checklists you can use. Stamp catalogs also can be helpful in showing you what stamps have been issued on a particular subject, but this could involve extensive research.

As you begin topical collecting, remember that you still are collecting stamps and the focus should be on the stamps rather than on the related items you choose to include in the collection.

Organizations like the American Topical Association have many useful publications and checklists that will make it easier for you to gauge the size of the task you are taking on when picking a topic to collect. Write to the association and find out what publications they have in your area of interest.

Some topical collectors are purists. That is, they insist that the subject being collected be the central theme of the stamp design. A collector of trees on stamps, for instance, would insist that the tree be the dominant feature of the stamp design. Others who want a broader collection would include in it stamps on which the tree appears at the side of a building or elsewhere in the background.

Collections of medicine on stamps can include everything from a stamp showing a picture of a noted doctor—such as the Walter Reed issue of the United States—to stamps that show hospitals, progress in medicine, or even the plants and herbs from which medicines are derived.

Before discussing some specialized approaches to topical

collecting, a word of caution. If you stick to stamps issued by countries with a legitimate reason to issue them you will have a collection that will cost a lot less and will have a more solid standing in the philatelic world. Avoid countries that issue overpriced stamps and souvenir sheets simply to capitalize on collector interest. Many countries issued "Kennedy" stamps simply because they knew collectors would buy them. That was the limit of their interest in Kennedy or the United States.

This problem has been particularly evident in the case of space on stamps, where many countries issued stamps and souvenir sheets with their only connection to space exploration being the fact that they were located on the earth over which the space flights passed. Such issues often are very colorful and bright and tempt many collectors. If you want such items in your collection, that is up to you. But you should purchase them with the full awareness that they probably will never be worth what you paid for them and that their resale value is virtually nil.

Without attempting to cover the broad field of topical collecting any further, let's look at a few areas where books have been written about a particular kind of topical collecting. Such books offer interesting glimpses into the world they represent in addition to providing information about the stamps covering the particular theme. The examples given are by no means complete. They are merely a sampler of what is available and should serve as a stepping stone for you in finding out more about the topic in which you are interested.

In 1978, the National Council of Teachers of Mathematics produced a book called *Mathematics and Science*, by William L. Schaaf. It begins by telling us that mathematics has a history of its own, just as science or art has, and that—like the story of other human achievements—the story has been told on postage stamps.

The book provides a broad interpretation of what stamps should or could be included in a collection focused on mathematics. The stamps included range from those recalling ancient beginnings to modern space flight.

On the ancient side we have the Algerian stamp of 1964 showing an ancient Egyptian war chariot with Ramses II battling the Hittites. It is typical of the chariots of Babylonia, Egypt, and Assyria, and shows that the wheel already was in common use.

Leaping rapidly forward we come to Gerardus Mercator of Flanders, one of the outstanding mapmakers of his age. His efforts produced the "Mercator projections" of 1569, which made possible much more realistic measurement of distances on the earth's surface. One of his maps is shown on a Canadian stamp of 1898.

United States stamps that would fit into a collection of this type include the Atoms for Peace issue of 1955; the 1962 commemorative honoring Senator Brien McMahon for his role in opening the way to the peaceful uses of atomic energy; and the 1949 airmail stamp honoring the Wright Brothers and their first successful flight in a motor-powered airplane. Australian stamps of 1973 show metric conversion.

Stamps showing anything from an abacus to a radio telescope could reasonably be included in a collection of this type.

As further discussion of topical collecting is provided you will note that a stamp in one collection also could logically appear in several other collections. The map stamps in the mathematics collection could also go in a collection of maps on stamps, or a collection of scientific milestones on stamps.

Medicine is another popular topical. In 1970 the American Medical Association issued a publication called *Medicine on Stamps*. It combines some history of medicine with samples of stamps featuring medical subjects.

Tradition has it that Asklepios was removed by Apollo from his mother's womb after she had been slain. The child was placed in the care of the centaur Chiron, who taught him botany and the effectiveness of plants in healing.

Asklepios was himself slain by Zeus, who later relented and elevated him to the godhead of medicine. It is the serpent-entwined staff of Asklepios that became the symbol of medicine. He is shown on a 1948 stamp from Spain.

United States stamps that would fit into this collection include the 1948 issue honoring Clara Barton, founder of the American Red Cross, Dr. Walter Reed, and the famous nurse, Clara Maass, who was the subject of a 1976 commemorative. In 1964 the U.S. honored the Mayo brothers, William and Charles, and their famous clinic.

Also included could be the 1959 tribute to Dr. Ephraim McDowell, who performed the first successful ovarian operation in the United States, in 1809; and the 1956 commemorative honoring Harvey Washington Riley on the fiftieth anniversary of the passage of the Pure Food and Drug laws.

Other stamps in the medicine collection range from allergy to physiology.

Specialization in topical collecting is further refined in the 1956 book by Herbert Rosen called *Radio Philatelia*. Years before topical collecting became popular Rosen discovered that radio, and in a broader sense, telecommunications, would make an unusual and interesting philatelic subject.

A collection of this type would include the 1936 issue of Germany, which honored Otto von Guericke, the physicist who invented the first electrical generator.

United States issues suited to this type of collection would include the 1940 salute to Samuel F. B. Morse; the 1944 issue marking the one-hundredth anniversary of the first message to be transmitted by telegraph; the Thomas Edison stamps of 1947; and the 1929 issues showing the incandescent lamp.

Randle Bond Truett made a hobby out of Abraham Lincoln on stamps. He wrote a book in 1959 called *Lincoln in Philately*. It reviews the many times Lincoln has appeared on the stamps not only of the United States but of many other nations.

One of the more interesting stamps he describes is the fifteen-cent issue of 1866, which was issued just one year after Lincoln's death. Many collectors consider it to be a mourning stamp, although others classify it as a memorial or commemorative.

In addition to appearing on U.S. stamps, Lincoln has been featured on U.S. postal cards; these also could fit into a topical collection.

Some variations of this type of collecting can be found in the stamp societies that have sprung up during the administrations of various presidents including Eisenhower and Kennedy. Such a topical collection could include covers cancelled on dates significant to the president, such as inauguration, reelection, birthdays, and the like. Presidential franks—used by the president to indicate no postage is required—also belong in a collection of this kind. The stamps in such a collec-

COLLECTORS of ships on stamps had a special cachet to mark the first day in commission of the aircraft carrier John F. Kennedy. *This cover was prepared by the Ship Cancellation Society.*

JOHN F. KENNEDY *was the subject of many philatelic tributes, both at the time of his assassination in 1963 and on anniversaries since that tragedy. Some were elaborate, like the one prepared for approval by the President's widow, which carry a photograph selected by her. Some much simpler tributes included the pen-and-ink variety illustrated here.*

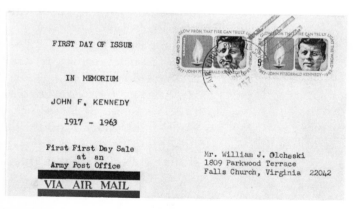

THIS COVER *notes the first-day of sale of the Kennedy stamps at an Army post office (APO).*

THE DALLAS *Philatelic Society produced this memorial cover in 1964.*

A PLATE NUMBER SINGLE is used to pay the postage on this "assassination anniversary" cover.

MANY FOREIGN governments issued philatelic tributes to the assassinated president. These are from West Germany and the Republic of Guinea.

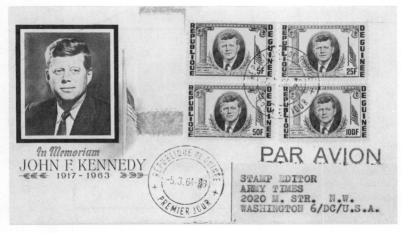

BY AIR MAIL

R 382 ٣٨٢ مصر.ش

In Memoriam
Sir Winston Churchill
1874-1965
100 NP

In Memoriam
Sir Winston Churchill
1874-1965
60 NP

In Memoriam
Sir Winston Churchill
1874-1965
40 NP

الشارقة

SHARJAH
FIRST DAY OF ISSUE

Stamp Editor, Army Times,
American Weekend,
2020 M St., N.W.,
Washington 6, D.C.,
United States.

THE MOST SERENE

REPUBLIC
OF SAN MARINO

IN MEMORY OF

John F. Kennedy

35ᵗʰ PRESIDENT

OF THE
UNITED STATES OF AMERICA

San Marino

22ⁿᵈ November, 1964
(1664 from the Foundation
of the Republic)

*FOREIGN NATIONS paid
tribute to Kennedy in
colorful fashion. San
Marino put its two
stamps in a souvenir
folder. Sharjah, on the
Arabian Peninsula,
found it had some
Kennedy stamps left
over, so it overprinted
them as a memorial to
Winston Churchill.*

Read & Advertise
in the
Precancel Stamp
Collector
Wildwood, N. J.

U.S. POSTAGE
WILDWOOD
DEC-2'63
N.J.
P.B.METER
476433
=05

*COLLECTORS of metered
mail got into the act
with this cover issued
by the Precancel
Stamp Society in De-
cember of 1963.*

WILDWOOD, N. J.

STAMP EDITOR
CAP & ARMY TIMES
2201 'M' STREET, N.W.
WASHINGTON 37, D.C.
20037

THE "COMPEX" *Stamp Show in Chicago in 1964 featured President Kennedy on its cacheted cover on the show's opening day and used the stamp to pay the postage.*

IN 1967 THE U.S. *issued a 13-cent definitive stamp showing President Kennedy. First-day ceremonies were at Brookline, Massachusetts.*

AN ELEVEN-CENT JFK *aerogramme was issued in 1965, and a 13-cent version in 1967.*

tion would be limited to foreign issues during the life of the president, since the United States does not issue stamps showing identifiable living persons.

HERE ARE JUST A FEW of the many Kennedy stamps issued by foreign countries.

No discussion of topical collecting would be complete without at least one more mention of space on stamps. This topic has attracted collectors around the world, and the recent slowdown in space exploration has done little to dim the

interest. Space on stamps is the Cadillac of topical collecting. The collections include souvenir sheets, special covers, and many other expensive items. There are catalogs and albums that cost hundreds of dollars.

Emery Kelen took an interesting look at this kind of collecting in 1972 in his book *Stamps Tell the Story of Space Travel*. As the author points out, "From Galileo to Goddard, from Copernicus to the Apollo flights, the exciting story of space travel has been memorialized in stamps issued by countries all over the world."

The subjects cover nearly every aspect of space exploration, including the early thinkers who formulated the first laws of planetary motion, the pioneers of rocketry, the teams of American astronauts, and Soviet cosmonauts.

Open a stamp album to any of the major countries and you will probably find stamps honoring a contribution to space exploration. Poland has a stamp for Nicholas Copernicus, who debunked the theory that Earth was the center of the universe. An Israeli stamp shows Johannes Kepler, who developed laws of planetary motion. Italy has philatelic coverage for Galileo, who built the first astronomical telescope, and Great Britain has stamps to honor Sir Isaac Newton, who scientifically explained the basic principle of rocket propulsion.

The United States can add a long list of its own space scientists on stamps—notably Robert H. Goddard, the rocket pioneer, who as early as 1919 produced a scientific paper that showed the possibility of a rocket reaching the moon.

Of course, the collecting of space topicals goes far beyond picturing the men who have made space history. Many countries have stamps picturing rockets, tracking stations, satellites, and various other space vehicles.

Even animals have their place in a space-on-stamps collection. The United States launched a rocket in 1961 with a chimpanzee passenger. That same year another chimp survived two orbits in a Mercury–Atlas V. Russia sent a dog into orbit, and one of the puppies from her next litter was presented to the White House when Kennedy was president. Rumania also sent a dog, Laika, into space. The dog—and a rabbit, who was also a space traveler—were later pictured on Romanian stamps.

The list of possible topical-collection themes is limitless. Open the encyclopedia and pick a subject. You will be able to build a topical collection around most any listing.

If you want fun, interest, and education through philately, topical collecting is the place to begin your search.

4

The Olympics

When U.S. athletes skated off with the gold medals in hockey and skating in the 1980 Winter Olympic Games at Lake Placid, New York, they gave a good boost not only to national pride and morale but to stamp collecting as well. Sales of the stamps depicting the various events soared as noncollectors competed with collectors to add the stamps to their souvenirs. Collecting Olympic stamps as a topical specialty is also likely to increase in popularity.

The modern Olympics began in Athens, Greece in 1896, with nine nations participating. The three Greek stamps shown here were part of the set issued to observe the games.

The United States provides an excellent start for an Olympics stamp collection. Below are some of the various U.S. issues of the past forty-eight years.

This 2-center was issued in 1932 to observe the International Winter Olympic Games at Lake Placid, N.Y. Printed in red ink and enclosed in a single-line border, the stamp was first placed on sale at Lake Placid on January 25, 1932.

The Summer Olympics of 1932 was held in Los Angeles from July 30 to August 14. The 3-cent stamp was printed in purple ink, the 5-center in blue. Both were first placed on sale at Los Angeles on June 15, 1932.

The VIII Olympic Winter Games were held at Squaw Valley, Calif., in 1960, and the U.S. issued a 4-cent stamp to mark the event. Above the stylized snowflake, the five entwined links represent the five continents, interlocked in the ancient symbol of eternal friendship. The stamp was first sold on February 18, 1960, at Tahoe City, Calif., and all first-day covers were postmarked "Olympic Valley, California," a U.S. Post Office station specially established at the site of the games to accommodate visitors.

By 1972 the U.S. was becoming more creative with its commemoratives; this was reflected in the four-stamp issue marking the XI Winter Olympics at Sapporo, Japan, and the XX Summer Olympics at Munich, Germany. Three of the stamps were surface mail, the 11-center air mail. All were issued in Washington, D.C., on August 17, 1972.

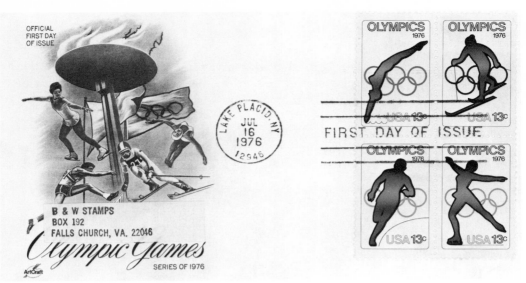

In 1976 four 13-cent stamps marked the XII Winter Olympics at Innsbruck, Austria, in February and the Summer Games at Montreal, Canada, in July. This issue was also designed to remind buyers of the Winter Games that would be held four years later at Lake Placid. All four stamps were issued at Lake Placid on July 16.

The United States went all out philatelically for the 1980 Winter Olympics, which took place at Lake Placid from February 12 to 24, and for the Summer Games, scheduled to be held in Moscow, USSR, from July 19 to August 3. The Soviet invasion of Afghanistan caused the United States to boycott the Summer Games. On March 11, 1980, the U.S. Postal Service decided to withdraw all of the 1980 Summer Olympic items from distribution, creating a run on the stamps as their interest and value to collectors increased.

The 1980 U.S. package was made up of ten commemoratives, three postal cards, an embossed envelope, and an aerogramme. Sports depicted were ski-jumping and downhill skiing; figure skating, ice hockey, and speed skating; sprinting, distance running, and high jumping; javelin- and discus-throwing; soccer, equestrian events, and gymnastics. The issues are shown below.

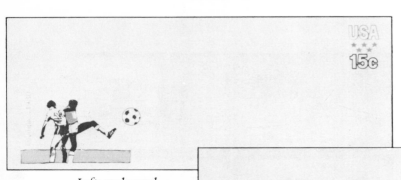

Left: embossed stamped 15-cent envelope, issued December 10, 1979, at East Rutherford, N.J. Right: discus throwing, another decathlon event, graced the 22-cent aerogramme.

Top: block of four 15-cent commemoratives honoring 1980 Winter Olympics were issued at Lake Placid on February 1, 1980; right: block of four 15-centers for 1980 Summer Games, issued at Los Angeles on September 28, 1979. Bottom left: airmail high jumper, issued November 1, 1979, at Colorado Springs, Colo. Bottom right: decathlon event adorned 10-cent domestic rate postcard commemorative.

Olympic issues, of course, are not limited to the United States. Many of the participating countries have issued commemoratives, semi-postals, and souvenir sheets over the years. Some are shown below.

Three commemorative postal cards for 1980 Games: domestic rate 10-center, issued September 17, 1979, at Eugene, Ore.: 14-cent international air mail card, released December 1, 1979, at Fort Worth, Tex.

Australia issued four stamps in 1956 to commemorate the XVI Olympic Games at Melbourne. The four-pence value shown here was the low value in the set. A souvenir sheet showing all four stamps was privately produced but never was valid for postage.

Hungary used six stamps in honor of the VIII Olympic Winter Games at Squaw Valley, Calif. in February 1960. Shown here is the low value in the set.

Seven stamps and a souvenir sheet were used by Hungary to publicize the IX Winter Olympics at Innsbruck, Austria, in January 1964. This stamp featured a skier. Others showed rifle shooting on skis and speed and figure skating.

Still another Hungarian issue was used to publicize the XVIII Olympic Games held in Tokyo in 1964. Illustrated are three stamps from the set which consisted of nine stamps.

Italy used a view of the stadium on one of its stamps to commemorate the VII Winter Olympic Games at Cortina d'Ampezzo January 26 to February 5, 1956. When the XVII Olympic Games came to Rome in 1960 nine stamps were issued. The 15-lire stamp shows a Roman Consul on the way to the games.

In 1953 Monaco issued six stamps to publicize its participation in the Helsinki Olympic Games. Other sports featured in the set included sailing, cycling, and gymnastics.

Fencing is featured on this stamp issued by Poland in 1956. The set of which it is a part commemorates the XVI Olympics which were held in Melbourne, Australia, November 22 through December 8, 1956.

Romanian issues that belong in an Olympic collection include these stamps found in sets issued for the Melbourne Olympics in 1956; the 1960 Olympics in Rome; and the 1964 Games in Innsbruck.

Rwanda, in Central Africa, issued eight stamps in 1964 to mark the XVIII Olympic Games in Tokyo, Japan.

San Marino used ten stamps and three souvenir sheets to salute the 1960 Games in Rome.

Togo, in West Africa, used seven stamps in a combination salute to the 1960 Winter Games at Squaw Valley and the Olympic Games in Rome.

Japan used semipostals to publicize the 1964 Olympics in Tokyo. The surcharge was used to defray expenses of the games.

Perhaps one of the most elaborate Olympic salutes was this souvenir sheet from West Germany. It was issued on July 5, 1972, to mark the XX Olympic Games in Munich. The sheet was actually made up of four stamps which could be detached from the sheet and used for postage. All were semipostals, with the surcharge used for the Foundation for the Promotion of the Munich Olympic Games. The stamps, together with the surrounding space on the sheet, gave a panoramic view of the game grounds.

It is, of course, obvious that the stamps illustrated in this chapter are just a few of those issued to commemorate Olympic activity around the world. It is not intended to be a comprehensive list, but is instead an effort to whet your appetite for further investigation of this exciting area of collecting.

5

The United Nations

Collecting the stamps of the United Nations offers an opportunity to enjoy many of the variations of stamp collecting and still stay within a controllable area. There are United Nations commemoratives, definitives, postal stationery, topicals, post cards, souvenir sheets, and other specialized items.

The idea of establishing the United Nations Postal Administration originally came from Dr. José Arce, head of the Argentine delegation to the UN in 1947. It was he who placed before the General Assembly on August 28, 1947, a draft resolution that eventually led to the signing of an agreement between the United Nations and the United States Post Office Department on March 28, 1951.

The first United Nations stamps went on sale later that year on United Nations Day, October 24, 1951. All of the stamps in the first series were definitives and airmails. The first commemorative UN stamps were issued in 1952 and it has been the UN practice to release about five commemorative stamps a year ever since.

By 1968 the success of the UN postal ventures in New York led to an agreement with the Swiss government for the issue and sale of United Nations stamps in Swiss denominations.

After a number of meetings with the Swiss government an agreement was signed making UNPA Geneva a post office in its own right; here, the new Swiss denomination stamps went on sale in 1969 with the release of eight definitives. Beginning in 1971 the commemoratives were issued in Swiss currency.

In August of 1979 United Nations Postal Administration offices were opened in Vienna, Austria, with stamps issued in Austrian currency. They were authorized for use only on mail posted at Donaupark Vienna International Center for the United Nations, and the Atomic Energy Agency.

United Nations stamps are valid for postage only when mailed from the United Nations headquarters in New York, the office in Geneva, and the designated offices in Austria.

During the first twenty-five years of UN issues, more than 954 million stamps and nearly 24 million pieces of postal stationery were printed for the United Nations by firms in Austria, Canada, Czechoslovakia, Finland, the Federal Republic of Germany, Greece, Japan, the Netherlands, Spain, Switzerland, Turkey, the United Kingdom, and the United States. The stamps were designed by artists from a panel of nearly 800 professional designers in more than fifty-eight countries. The artists participate in a world design competition for each issue.

Designs have also been reproduced from the works of Marc Chagall and Pablo Picasso.

ART AT THE UNITED NATIONS was featured in this 1967 UN souvenir sheet. The design focuses on "The Kiss of Peace," the stained-glass window by Marc Chagall. The sheet is divisible into six stamps, each rouletted on three sides and imperforate on the other. Slightly over 3 million of the sheets were produced, with 617,000 cancelled on the first day.

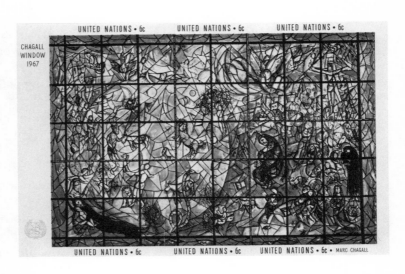

As a rule, postage stamps pay tribute to famous people or important events in a nation's history. This is not the case with stamps of the United Nations. Their purpose is to publicize United Nations activities, many of which affect our lives as world citizens. Some examples are peaceful uses of outer space, safety in the air, the fight against cancer, and the efforts to curb drug abuse.

Another factor making UN issues popular with many collectors is the limited printing. Commemorative stamps are printed in small quantities and are taken off sale after about a year in most cases. They are never reprinted.

Perhaps the most interesting United Nations issue is the first souvenir sheet. It was issued on October 24, 1955, to mark the tenth anniversary of the ratification of the United Nations Charter. The occasion was marked by the issue for the first time of a UN set in three values instead of the usual two, along with a souvenir sheet reproducing the three values.

One million copies of each of the stamps, in three-, four-, and eight-cent values were produced, but only 200,000 copies of the souvenir sheet were ordered. The United Nations didn't expect much demand for the sheet, since it was too large to use for postage. Events since that date have shown that the UN made a very bad guess on the degree of interest in the sheets.

Orders poured in to the UN Postal Administration before the sheet was issued, and a rationing system was instituted, giving some dealers only ten percent of the sheets they had ordered.

When the issue date arrived collectors created a record customer jam at the UN sales counter. Sales were limited to ten per collector, but many collectors went back in line and stood for hours to get more of the sheets.

Three days later a second printing of 50,000 was made to meet at least part of the demand. Sales on this printing were limited to one per customer, and again there were long lines as collectors got a sheet and then went back in line for another copy.

It was not until later that it was discovered that there were differences between the two printings.

Official records for the period say the paper was slightly different, the gum was heavier and more yellow. The more easily recognized difference was on the eight-cent denomination on the sheet, where a small white space could be seen under the letter "n" in the French word "Unies." This was corrected in the second printing and the white space was eliminated.

After the initial demand it was almost a year before the souvenir sheet began to shoot up in value. Today the sheets are worth hundreds of dollars and represent about half the total value of a United Nations mint collection.

THE FIRST UNITED NATIONS
ISSUES *were definitives
that appeared in 1951.
The designs featured
themes in which the
United Nations was
interested, as well as
various UN buildings.*

HUMAN RIGHTS DAY *in
1956 was marked by
the issue of a pair of
commemorative UN
stamps showing a
flame and a globe.*

THE UN CONFERENCE *on
Trade and Develop-
ment, held in Geneva
in 1964, inspired this
pair of commemora-
tives. The arrows show
the global flow of trade.*

AIRMAIL POSTAL CARD, *is-
sued by the United Na-
tions in 1966, was
printed in Scranton,
Pennsylvania.*

AIR MAIL POSTAL CARD

UNITED NATIONS · NATIONS UNIES

NEW YORK 10017

ОБЪЕДИНЕННЫЕ НАЦИИ
UNITED NATIONS · NATIONS UNIES
NACIONES UNIDAS

UNITED NATIONS
NEW YORK
JAN 19 PM 1979

MR BILL OLCHESKI
BOX 30
FALLS CHURCH VA
22046

LETTERS FROM THE UN con-taining new-issue in-formation often bear United Nations stamps and make an interest-ing addition to a col-lection.

METER CANCELLATIONS of-
ten are used on United
Nations mail. They fre-
quently include a slo-
gan cancellation, as
can be seen in this ex-
ample.

FIRST-DAY UN COVER bear-
ing the souvenir sheet
used to note the 20th
anniversary of the
world body.

There are a number of ways to acquire United Nations stamps. One way is to visit the philatelic sales counters at UN offices in New York, Geneva, or Vienna. In addition to selling stamps the counters offer souvenir cards, postal stationery, stamp sets, souvenir folders, and posters.

Stamps and other items also may be ordered by mail. Such orders should be addressed to the United Nations Postal Administration, Box 5900, Grand Central Station, New York, NY 10017.

There is also an easy, automatic way to collect United Nations stamps and to receive publicity material in advance of the issue dates of the stamps. This is done by establishing a deposit account with a minimum deposit of twenty dollars. New stamps then are sent as issued until the deposit is exhausted; it must then be renewed if you want to continue getting the stamps. There is an added advantage in using this method: it usually guarantees that you will receive copies of issues that may suddenly become scarce and shoot up in value.

Write to the UN Postal Administration at the New York address and request details on what is available. This will get you on the mailing list to receive information about future issues. As a bonus, the United Nations uses UN stamps on its mailings of the informational releases, giving you some interesting covers for your collection.

One of the other advantages in collecting stamps of the United Nations is that you can get a complete collection for a few hundred dollars—if you are willing to do without the expensive souvenir sheet.

Even if you decide not to try to get all of the issues, consider adding a few UN items to your collection. They are interesting, colorful, and fun to collect.

Philatelic
Message Carriers

Stamps and cancellations are often used to carry messages of social concern. Collecting stamps and cancels of this type provides an interesting variation to your topical collection.

The United States makes effective use of stamp themes to focus on the environment, natural resources, conservation, energy, and various health topics.

In March 1971 the United States issued a commemorative promoting blood donation. The American Association of Blood Banks says issue of this stamp increased blood donations enough to replenish blood bank shortages for about six months. In 1968 there was a stamp urging Americans to register and vote. A 1965 commemorative called attention to traffic safety, another to the cancer crusade stressing that early diagnosis can save lives. The Law and Order theme was publicized in 1968, and there were 1974 stamps asking us to preserve the environment and to help retarded children. Energy conservation was the subject of several issues. The campaign against drug abuse was the theme of a 1971 issue.

Other stamps that would fit into a collection of this type include the Freedom from Hunger issue of 1963, the stamp urging employment of the handicapped in 1960, and the forest conservation commemorative of 1958.

A message of another kind was featured in the 1980 stamps issued as part of the observance of National Letter Writing Week. This unusual issue consisted of three pairs of stamps. Each pair included one large and one small stamp.

All of the designs were repeated on the panes. The three larger stamps each carried a different message. Messages were: "Letters Lift Spirits"; "Letters Preserve Memories"; and "Letters Shape Opinions." Paired with each of the larger stamps was a smaller stamp bearing the request: "P.S. Write Soon." The arrangement was made more interesting to collectors by having each of the smaller stamps in different colors. The color in the smaller stamp complemented the color of the larger stamp to which it was paired.

Slogan cancellations are often used to promote social causes. They are a particularly popular approach with various health organizations. Collectors interested in cancellations of this type can either collect one example of each cancellation—and there are hundreds of varieties—or they can try to collect the same cancellation as it is used in different cities. Some cancellations, like the ones identifying an "All-America City" may be used in only one city, while others, like "Pray for Peace" may be used in hundreds of cities.

The charity types such as those illustrated here are used in many cities.

Postmarks, like slogans, are inexpensive to acquire and fun to collect. They also give you a chance to let your imagination play games.

Consider, for instance, these postmarks as identifiers of various types of personality:

You might try to find your own name on a cancellation. Here are a few girl and boy names for openers:

LEWIS, IA
JUL 11 1979 PM
51544

USA 15c
Seeing For Me

STELLA, MO
JUL 10 PM 1979
64867

USA 15c
Seeing For Me

GARY, IN
JUL 12 PM 1979
464

ADA, KS
JUL 20 P.M. 1979
67414

USA 15c

VERNON
JUL 11 1979
47282

USA 15c

CLARENCE, IL
JUL 11 PM
60925

Auto Racing
USA 15c

MARION
JUL 17 PM 1979
1723

USA 15c

ADRIAN, OR
AUG 10 1979
97901

USA 15c

LILY, SD
JUL 10 PM 1979
57250

USA 15c

CALVIN, ND
JUL 9 AM 1979
58323

USA 15c

IRVING, IL
JUL 26 PM 1979
62051

15c
HOME OF THE BRAVE

ALEXANDER, ND
JUL 12 1979 PM
58831

USA 15c
HOME OF THE BRAVE

Collectors can find almost as many topics in postmarks as they can in stamps. Suppose, for instance, you wanted to collect chemical elements on postmarks. Here are a few with which you could begin:

If you prefer a "wearing apparel" topical, try:

"Indians on Postmarks" could include the following samples:

You can even put together messages like this sequence:

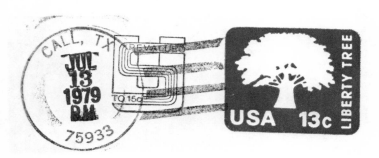

As you can see, there are no limits to the fun you can have with postmarks, cancellations and slogans. The samples illustrated in this chapter are designed to whet your appetite for further discoveries.

The fun you have might not carry you to:

But one thing is certain. If you continue working on your stamp collection your morale will:

7

Picking a Stamp Dealer

Pick your stamp dealer with the same care that you pick your stamp album. The right choice can lead to a pleasant and profitable relationship that can last for years. The wrong choice can make each transaction a confrontation.

A good relationship with one or more stamp dealers increases your enjoyment of the hobby. They can help you find the stamps you need, provide you with supplies, tell you about local clubs, introduce you to other collectors, and even add spice to your evenings with an occasional stamp auction.

Stamp dealers, like stamp albums, come in many types. They range from the vest-pocket variety working out of the corner of a basement to the big-time operators with dozens of employees.

There are about three thousand full-time and ten thousand part-time dealers in the United States.

In picking a dealer, as in picking an album, look for one most closely meeting your needs. Those needs will vary depending on the direction you want to pursue in your collecting and the access you have to stamps and philatelic supplies. If you are in a metropolitan area, you will have the pick of many dealers. In a small town, you may have only one dealer, or you may have to do your own stamp business by mail.

Approach your search for a dealer with the same caution you use in selecting a mechanic or a television repairman. Ask other collectors about firms with which they have done business.

Here are a few of the key things you will want to know about a dealer:

■ Does the firm carry a full line of the kind of stamps in which you are interested? Some dealers specialize in stamps of the United States, others in the stamps of foreign nations. Still others carry the full range of worldwide stamps.

■ If the dealer has a shop, is it open at hours convenient to you? Some dealers only work part time and thus are open only in the evenings or on weekends. This could be a problem if you are retired or work evening hours, and need to have a dealer who operates on a schedule more in keeping with your own.

■ Does the dealer sell primarily stamps and philatelic supplies? Some stamp dealers turn out to be hobby shops where you have to line up behind the youngsters waiting to buy goldfish food. Further, such a dealer probably knows more about goldfish than about stamps, and will be of little help to you if you have technical questions.

■ Does the dealer offer philatelic material at a wide range of price levels? Some dealers specialize in higher-priced items and consider it a waste of time to deal with beginners or those with limited stamp budgets who are interested mainly in packets and job lots.

Visit one or more local stamp clubs and discuss the relationship local dealers have with them. Does the dealer ever show up at club meetings as a guest speaker? This would make good business sense for the dealer since it would bring him new customers. But, many dealers are "too busy" for this kind of activity.

You will want to know if the dealer keeps a current supply of supplements, catalogs, and other updating materials. If a dealer sells you an album, that dealer should be prepared to supply you with supplements as they are issued each year. If your local dealer has a reputation for being negligent in keeping current on such items, find another dealer.

Conversations with club members and other collectors also will let you know if the dealer is interested in people. This can be important. The dealer who wants to know what you collect—who goes out of the way to look up information for you, who calls you when an interesting item comes in stock—can become a good friend as well as a source of stamps and supplies.

If the dealer has a shop, you will want to know if the surroundings are comfortable. This does not mean you need to have overstuffed chairs and fancy quarters (in fact, if the place is too fancy, you can be sure this will be reflected in the prices asked for stamps). It does mean there should be adequate lighting; ample room to spread out an album; comfortable chairs; and a supply of catalogs, price lists, and other reference material.

On your first visit to a stamp dealer, ask about pricing policies used by the firm. Not all dealers follow the same policy not even those that might be located next door to each other. Check with other collectors who have had dealings with the firm and ask them if they considered the prices charged reasonable for the quality of stamps received. Some dealers use standardized price lists, such as the "Brookman's," which you will find in many stamp shops. This is published several times a year and is a generally accepted price guide in many areas. Some dealers base prices on a percentage of catalog value; others charge whatever they think the traffic will bear.

It is also a good idea to become familiar with a dealer's views on *condition* of stamps. There is an old joke in the stamp trade that says whatever I sell to you is in "fine" condition and whatever you sell to me is in "average" condition. Condition, of course, has a great impact on the price of stamps. A stamp in "fine" condition could cost twice as much or more than one in "average" condition and still be a bargain. A conversation with the dealer on the first visit should clarify definitions of condition used by the firm.

Here are some considerations dealers use when classifying a stamp by condition:

■ Is the stamp discolored, faded, or stained?
■ How is the centering? Is the design evenly placed between the edges of the stamp?
■ Are the perforations intact? That is, have they been damaged when the stamps were separated?
■ Is the gum cracked or otherwise disturbed? Has the stamp ever been hinged (in the case of a mint stamp)? Some dealers will not consider rating a stamp as "fine" if it has ever been hinged—no matter how good the other features may be.

This emphasis on condition is justified. It is particularly true of older stamps where prime condition commands premium prices. In more recent issues—covering the last twenty years or so—anything below "fine" condition causes the stamp to be considered of minimal value. Ask your dealer about the importance of condition and the role it plays in his pricing policies. The conversation will be enlightening for you and could set ground rules for your future transactions with the dealer.

Dealers can be helpful only if you let them. Some collectors resent dealer interference in their browsing, and this discourages dealers from getting too closely involved with the customers.

If you tell your dealer the approximate size of your monthly hobby budget, he or she is in a much better position to advise you on your purchases. Suppose you want to spend twenty-five dollars a month on stamps. Would it be smarter to put it all in one stamp or in a variety of stamps? Your dealer can help you decide—but only if he or she knows how far along you are in your collection and how far and how fast you eventually hope to go.

If you intend to collect as an investment, the dealer can show you price trends and help you pick the best buys at any given time. The Wholesale Price Index tells grocers where prices are going to be in a couple of months. The price a stamp dealer pays for replacement stock gives him a pretty good indication of what will be increasing in price when the new price lists are published. Dealers are not reluctant to share this information with you if you are a regular customer. Of course, investing is a gamble and there is no guarantee that such investment advice will always be correct.

The ultimate value of a stamp—or of any other investment—is what some other person will pay to own the item or part of the project. Some of the souvenir sheets of the Persian Gulf countries illustrate this point. They have catalog values that make them look like great investments. However, there is a slight problem. Few collectors want them. So, you may be holding a sheet that has a "book value" of twenty dollars, but you may have a hard time finding a collector who will give you more than two or three dollars for it.

Dealers can help you when you want to dispose of all or part of a collection. This is discussed in detail elsewhere in the book so will not be dealt with at great length here. Suffice it to say that dealers will buy almost any philatelic material you have to sell if the price is right. They will buy it *now* and they will pay you cash. You probably could get a better price if you sold to another collector, but the other collector may not have the ready cash or the interest in the entire collection.

If you have a highly specialized collection, your search for a suitable dealer may take a bit more time. Begin by seeing if your local dealers have any material of interest to you. This can be determined in a hurry by asking about specific items. "Do you have any stampless covers?" or "Do you have any French railway cancels?" or "What do you have in U.S. revenues?" will soon let you know if the dealer is going to be able to supply your specialized needs. It will also give you an indication of dealer attitude. Some will simply say: "Sorry, we don't carry those." Others will take the time to give you the name, address, and phone number of some other dealer who might have the items you want. Friendly dealers also may recommend specialist societies you might want to learn more about. You might even be given the names of other collectors in the area who share your interests.

Dealers can order most any stamp or philatelic item you need. They are in contact with suppliers all over the world and can get quick response to their queries by writing a dealer with whom they regularly do business. You might not get as fast a response if you wrote as an individual collector.

You might want to ask your dealer about credit policy. Some dealers accept major credit cards; some will consider payment plans, some have layaway plans, and some want cash on the barrelhead. This information could be important to you, particularly if you are interested in some major items and lack the cash to pay for them all at once.

Up until now we have been talking about finding a dealer in the local community. This is not possible for everyone. Small towns or lack of philatelic interest in an area may mean you do not have access to a local dealer. In such a case, you may want to consider the mail-order dealer.

Pick up a copy of one of the major philatelic publications at the library and look at the ads. The bigger publications have dozens of pages of such listings in each issue. Read them carefully and select the ones that appear most likely to meet your needs. Write to them, asking for general information about each firm and the way it does business.

Many mail-order dealers are "vest-pocket" operators. Each customer is important to them and they will put forth some extra effort to keep you as a customer.

You can get an impression of a dealer by the way in which your first letter is answered. If all you get back is the stamps you ordered, the effect is the same as buying stamps from a vending machine. The stamps are there. The value may be, too. But there is no concern on the part of the vendor about whether you ever make another purchase.

A mail-order dealer who knows your interests—plus the approximate size of your stamp budget and the time you have to spend on your collection—could become a friendly, helpful correspondent. This does not mean a pen pal. The part-time dealer who is trying to run a stamp business along with keeping a regular job doesn't have time to write long letters. But you can develop a relationship in which the dealer drops you a card about some stamps he or she has acquired, tells you about some new issues that may be of interest to you, mentions that a new album has been produced in your area of specialization. Smart dealers will solicit your "want lists" and will work to fill them promptly and at reasonable prices.

Another good place to look over stamp dealers and their services is at stamp shows. Major shows have dozens of dealers. Local shows may have only five or six. Many of the so-called "shows" are nothing more than a collection of dealers offering their wares from rented table space. Such groupings, called *bourses*, give you a chance to visit with a number of dealers in a short time, determine the quantity and quality of their offerings, gain an awareness of their pricing policy, and have a quick glimpse at their general attitude toward collectors.

Some of the dealers at the shows will have price lists or other publications, and will be compiling mailing lists for them. If you find any of interest, add your name and address to the list. There usually is no charge for this service.

Many dealers provide "approval" services; they are covered elsewhere in this book.

What kind of dealer is for you? That choice, like the choice of an album, ultimately must be made by you, and must be tailored to your individual needs. Start slowly and buy in small amounts until you are sure that what is promised is what is delivered. You soon will see if the stamps provided are in good condition, if they are delivered promptly, and if the dealer does not always seem to be "sold out" of the bargain items mentioned in the ads.

How close a relationship you have with a dealer is up to you. You may want an impersonal relationship. If so, limit your contact to sending orders and checks. If you want a closer relationship, put a personal note in with your next order and see the reaction you get.

Stamp collectors collect for fun. Stamp dealers sell to make money. There are a few dealers who combine the two. If you are lucky, you will find one who can see beyond the immediate dollar, and you both will benefit.

8

First-Day Covers

When the United States issues a new stamp it times the release dates to coincide with some date connected with the individual, the event, or the location being commemorated. The new stamps then are placed on sale at one or more post offices near the site connected with the stamp. The stamps are sold only at such post offices on the first day of issue. The following day they are placed on sale at post offices throughout the country.

The post office in the "first-day city" or cities gets to use a special cancellation that reads: "First Day of Issue." Envelopes to which the new stamps have been affixed and to which such cancellation has been applied are called "First-Day Covers."

Stamp columns and stamp publications regularly list the issue dates and sites of both United States and foreign stamps.

How popular is first-day cover collecting? The Washington Press, producers of the popular Artcraft First Day Covers, has a mailing piece on first-day covers in which they list some figures from the U.S. Postal Service to show the level of interest. In 1970, when the six-cent "Landing of the Pilgrims" stamp was released, there were 629,850 first-day covers cancelled. The following year there were 720,035 Douglas MacArthur first-day covers cancelled; and, in 1972, there were 847,500 of the eight-cent Yellowstone National Park FDCs serviced and almost two million of the American Colonial Craftsmen quartet of commemoratives.

The first recorded effort to get United States stamps specially cancelled on their first day of sale came with the 1898 Trans-Mississippi issue. First-day covers before that time were commercial covers that just happened to be used on the first day of issue without any philatelic identification. It is remarkable how many such covers survive today and are in the hands of collectors.

On those early covers, the only way to identify a first-day cover is to match the date of the cancellation with the issue date. In later years, decorated envelopes, usually with printed or rubber-stamped "cachets," were used for the covers, and identified the site of the first-day sales. The first cacheted first-day cover was created in 1923 for the Harding memorial stamp.

Modern covers have a cachet imprinted on the left side of the envelope. The design generally shows some event or feature related to the subject honored on the stamp.

First-day covers are collected in many variations, generally limited only by the imagination of the collector. The chief restriction on the stamps to be used on first-day covers in the United States is that the face value must be at least equal to the first-class letter rate.

THE USUAL WAY to collect U.S. first-day covers is with a single stamp. This cover has added interest since it was created for the Scandinavian Collectors Club in observance of Leif Erikson Day, which also was the issue date of the stamp.

LEIF ERIKSON DAY
OCTOBER 9, 1968
SCANDINAVIAN COLLECTORS CLUB

FIRST DAY OF ISSUE

B & W STAMP CO.
BOX 192
FALLS CHURCH, VA. 22046

The most commonly collected variety carry a single copy of the new stamp, unless there is more than one design on a pane, in which case sufficient stamps are affixed to complete the design.

Some collectors like to get a cover with a block of four, even though only one design is used. Others choose to collect a plate block. This type of collecting has been complicated in recent years by the use of multiple plate numbers, making it difficult to get the entire plate block on a standard-size envelope.

WHEN A DESIGN is spread over more than one stamp, the first-day cover generally includes the entire set.

Stamps of the United Nations usually are issued in a set of three or more and these generally are applied to one envelope for first-day cancellation. The UN also issues "inscription blocks" and souvenir sheets, which also make attractive first-day covers.

"ZIP" and "Maily Early" blocks add further interest to first-day covers of U.S. issues.

If your collection includes coil stamps it is a good idea to use a pair of the stamps in franking the covers sent in for first-day cancellation. This can be refined further by the use of line pairs—two coil stamps with a colored line running along the perforations between the stamps.

When booklet panes are submitted for first-day cancellation the entire pane is used, including the selvage.

First-day cancellations also may be obtained in the United States on postal stationery, stamped envelopes, postal cards, and aerogrammes.

Ground rules for first-day collecting have evolved through the years. Before 1929 there were few cachets. Often

they were made with a rubber stamp, had poor designs, and were frequently smudged. The first modern cachets appeared in the early 1920s but had limited usage. Collectors didn't mind if the covers were addressed; in fact, they expected them to be, and the size of the envelope was not of major concern. The basic demand as far as cachets were concerned was that they be readable. This practice prevailed into the mid-1930s.

Cachets became more popular about the same time, but they were still the exception rather than the rule. Addressed covers were still generally accepted.

Collectors began to get more particular as we entered the 1940s. Good centering was demanded and the cachets had to be clear and neat. After 1937 almost all U.S. first-day covers included the words "First Day of Issue" in the cancellation. About this time there was a switch to the use of the standard-size (6¾) envelopes for first-day covers.

Beginning early in the 1940s cachets were produced by many companies, and covers without cachets brought lower prices. Addresses were put on in pencil, or peelable labels were used and removed before the covers were added to the collections.

Collecting standards are more clearly defined for covers of the last twenty-five years. Envelopes have to be of standard size and made of quality paper. Cachets are mandatory and covers must be unaddressed.

There are many varieties of first-day covers produced every time a new stamp is issued. There could be dozens of different cachets. There also are variations in the cancellations, ranging from the machine variety to elaborate ones used for stamp shows and for cancelling stamps on covers other than envelopes. These "hand cancel" varieties are generally available in smaller quantities. They make interesting additions to any first-day cover collection.

The passage of time increases the value of the earlier covers. Of course, there can never be more first-day covers than the number cancelled during the issue period.

About 90 percent of all first-day covers are collected by individuals, the rest by dealers. Fleetwood, a major supplier of cacheted first-day covers, estimates a turnover of about 20 percent a year in first-day cover collections. It is this turnover that becomes the major source of supply of older covers to new collectors.

While there are no reliable statistics available, it is likely that the number of people who start collecting first-day covers and then stop is probably larger than the number who start stamp collecting and then give it up. Some stop because they lose interest, others don't want to make the investment required as cover makers keep coming up with fancier products and the prices increase. In some instances, the collections are part of estates and are broken up when the original collector dies.

A problem through the years has been the difficulty in selling a first-day-cover collection at a reasonable price. As a result, many have disappeared in attics, been misplaced or thrown away, or accidentally destroyed, gradually lessening the supply. Cover dealers estimate that about one fourth of all first-day covers disappear within five years of issue.

The number of collectors seemed to decrease, judging by the number of first-day cancels on issues, between 1948 and 1968. There was renewed interest beginning about 1970 as new companies entered the cachet field. This has caused collectors to want to go back and get the earlier issues. The higher prices they are willing to pay have brought many collections out of hiding and into the market.

Collectors of U.S. first-day covers have a choice of options in ordering their cancellations. They can wait until the stamps are issued, purchase them at the post office, affix them to their envelopes, and then forward them to the postmaster in the first-day city. No additional payment is required. The postmasters apply the first-day cancellation and return the cover to the collector. Such orders generally have to be submitted within two weeks of the issue date.

Collectors who want the Postal Service to affix the stamps—and this was the only way to get first-day cancellations until recent years—send addressed envelopes, plus the cost of the stamps to be affixed, to the postmaster in the first-day city, and the envelopes are stamped, cancelled, and returned.

Write the address legibly in pencil, which can be erased, or on a peelable label. The Postal Service would prefer to have you use the former method since this saves the time needed to affix the stamps and handle the payments. In fact, U.S. post offices have been instructed to give preferential handling to covers submitted already stamped.

Getting first-day covers from foreign countries is a bit more complicated. Some countries, like Canada, add a service charge to the cost of the stamp when processing first-day cancellation requests. The United Nations also makes an extra charge for first-day cancellations.

Foreign first-day covers are popular with first-day cover collectors because of the attractive designs and the elaborate

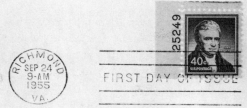

AN INTERESTING *variation is added to this first-day cover by the use of a plate number single stamp.*

SWEDISH *first-day cover.*

CANADIAN *first-day cover with inscriptions in English and French.*

presentations on the covers. Some countries provide a subscription service which makes it possible to establish a "deposit account" that pays for covers as they are issued; the covers are sent to you automatically.

Collectors who process their own covers may elect to buy cacheted envelopes from stamp dealers. Companies such as Artcraft produce attractive covers and these are available from many stamp dealers.

Some collectors prefer to design their own cachets. These range from drawings to photographs, to geometric patterns, or to whatever approach strikes the fancy of the collector.

If you want to prepare your own cachets, use a standard-size envelope addressed to yourself. Be sure the cachet you design is placed far enough to the left to allow room for the stamps and the address, particularly if you are going to have a block or a booklet pane affixed. Place the prepared envelopes in another envelope addressed to the postmaster in the first-day city. As explained earlier, you can either stamp the inner envelope at the time of mailing, or you can enclose remittance to cover the cost of stamps desired.

While these individually prepared covers add interest to a collection, they are not considered desirable by many collectors and would be valued at a price lower than those carrying commercially prepared cachets.

WHEN A FIRST-DAY COVER is desired on a stamp designed for a specific service—such as special delivery—the cover must also carry the prevailing first-class rate.

First-day covers usually are displayed in albums especially designed for them. These generally have plastic pockets that hold two covers per pocket. The pockets can be easily flipped to display either cover. One such holder, available from White Ace, holds 100 covers. White Ace also makes Allsyte albums designed to hold commercial size and other odd-shaped covers.

BOOKLET PANE *of the 1970 Eisenhower stamps on a first-day cover.*

OFFICIAL FDC *of the 7th FIQ World Bowling Tournament.*

STAMPED ENVELOPE *from the 1964 World's Fair, issued at the fair in New York on April 22.*

⑨
Stamp Auctions

As your collecting interests begin to expand you will also want to expand the sources you have for acquiring stamps for your collection. This is a good time to explore stamp auctions. Sales of this type come in many varieties and sizes. They range from the small auction held in the local stamp shop right up through major international auctions in which stamps worth many thousands of dollars change hands.

Auction buying is a good way to acquire stamps when a number of conditions prevail. Perhaps you have exhausted all local sources and still cannot locate the items you need. Perhaps your local dealer does not carry the specialized material in which you are interested. Or, you may just be the kind of person who enjoys the excitement of attending an auction and joining in the competitive bidding.

In dealing with stamp auctions there are steps you can take that will increase your chances for making a good deal. First, arrive at the auction site early and look over the items to be offered. Even small stamp-club auctions usually have the items to be sold on display before the meeting. Examine the stamps for damage, thin spots, heavy cancels, and other aspects of condition that would diminish their value. Be wary of stamps that are beautifully sealed in plastic mounts but cannot be turned over or otherwise examined for damage.

Next, look around at the competition. Who else in the group is likely to be bidding on the same items in which you are interested? This is not hard to determine. Just listen to the conversation around the auction table as the lots are examined. Be particularly alert to unpopular or highly specialized material in the auction. You may be able to pick up these lots without much competition and then resell them in another auction that has a bigger crowd or more specialists among the bidders.

Know ahead of time how much money you are prepared to spend, and on how many lots you want to bid. If you are especially interested in one lot, save your money until that lot is offered. Note in advance if a minimum bid is required and then decide how far above that amount you are prepared to go.

There is, unfortunately, no yardstick you can use to tell you how high a price any given lot will finally bring. Sometimes inexperienced collectors in the crowd get caught up in the excitement of the auction and bid out of proportion to the value of the items offered.

Auctions are places where you can sell as well as buy. The firm handling the sale will make a charge for its services, usually a percentage of the price realized, but there may also be a minimum charge.

Another type of auction you will want to know about is the mail-order auction. This is a system in which dealers gather a large group of lots and then publish an auction catalog that is mailed to many collectors. The catalog describes the items to be sold, the condition of the material, the approximate value, and the minimum bid that will be considered. Collectors mail in their bids—no money is sent—and the bids are gathered at the auction firm until the day of the sale. On that day, the mail bids are handled by a teller during the floor action. The sale begins with the auctioneer reading off the lot number from the catalog and announcing the starting bid. Bidders in the room make their offers and the person handling the mail bids raises the bids in accordance with directions received from the mail customer.

When you receive a catalog for a mail sale, read the terms that usually are outlined in the first page or two. They will tell you the increments in which bids must be made. For ex-

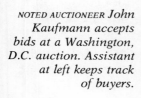

NOTED AUCTIONEER John Kaufmann accepts bids at a Washington, D.C. auction. Assistant at left keeps track of buyers.

ample, on the first ten dollars, bids must be raised at least fifty cents; on the next twenty-five dollars bids must be in increments of at least one dollar; on lots above fifty dollars, bids must be in increments of $2.50, and so on. The terms will also state whether the commission is paid by the buyer or the seller, and will explain the procedure for returning material which is not as advertised.

When bidding in mail auctions, do not be misled by the "value" placed on the items in the auction catalog. Sometimes this represents wishful thinking on the part of the seller. If you are interested in bidding in mail auctions, look at the ads in stamp publications and write to the auction houses for their catalogs. Sometimes such firms make a small charge for the catalogs, but the price then usually includes a followup summary that shows the actual prices for which the lots were sold—and this is where you should begin your research. Compare the "values" listed in the original auction catalog with the actual prices realized. You soon will decide whether the suggested values are realistic or merely an effort to encourage higher bids.

When you submit a bid in a mail sale, this is supposed to be the highest price you are willing to pay for the item. The floor representative will have your bid, along with many others, and is supposed to raise the bid each time until he buys the item or reaches the limit you are willing to offer. Thus, you might say you are willing to pay up to ten dollars for a given item. But, if the last highest bid is seven dollars, the floor representative should raise the bid by the next increment (assume fifty cents in this case) and the item should be sold to you for $7.50.

The firms that run mail auctions do so on a regular basis, so it is not difficult to determine the patterns they follow. Talk with other collectors who bid in mail auctions and exchange notes with them about how good and how honest the auction firm is. You will soon develop a list of reliable firms with which you might want to deal.

In a major auction, there is another element in addition to the floor bids and those received by mail. That is the telephone bid. If you were to attend a major sale, you might see a scene like this:

The auctioneer announces that the next lot consists of a rare Civil War cover, franked from some obscure town in West Virginia. He then says: "I have an opening bid of thirty dollars." Since the item has attracted considerable attention, the bidding will be spirited. The thirty-dollar bid is soon up to fifty dollars and the excitement begins to grow.

COVERS from two auction catalogs.

The people in the room generally fall into three categories: the collectors who have come hoping to find a bargain; the curious; and a few commercial buyers or collectors' representatives. The latter are the easiest to spot as they will be in the first row, will carry big briefcases, and will have catalogs and note papers spread out in front of them on the table. Once the initial flurry or bidding slows, the professionals move in, particularly if they feel the bidding is still well below the value of the item.

These professionals are known to the auctioneer and their bidding may be in the form of tilting a pencil, pulling an ear or closing a book. The auctioneer recognizes these signals and adjusts the announced bid accordingly. As the bidding progresses the excitement increases and the smaller bidders begin to drop out. Now it comes down to two or three bidders, and the bids are careful and deliberate. Just about the time it seems that bidding has ended on a particularly desirable item, a door at the back of the room opens slightly and a man holding a phone motions to the auctioneer, indicating that a prospective buyer on the phone wants to enter the competition. The bidding gets fast and furious. Suddenly, the door closes. The phone bidder has given up. In another few moments only one bidder remains and the hammer bangs down indicating a sale.

Some stamp stores have auctions on a regular basis. Check newspaper ads on the hobby page in your area. Such stores generally use a system in which customers are assigned a number they can use, either as buyers or sellers. The stores have preprinted auction sheets on which the lots to be sold are described and mounted. At the bottom of each page there is a space for the description of the lot, the catalog numbers, the number of the seller, the minimum bid, and the increments in which bids are accepted.

The lots to be offered on a given night are placed in a loose-leaf notebook, which is then left on the counter for a fixed period, generally a week or two before the auction. On auction night, the items are offered to the customers in the store who compete against the last bid registered on the auction sheet.

There will be some sheets on which no bid is received. This could occur because the asking price is too high or because the item is too specialized and was not seen by any interested collectors. Such lots are placed in what is called a "next-bid book" and are sold to whomever will bid one increment above the asked price. Lots not sold are returned to the seller.

Not all auctions are that involved, nor do they all deal with items of great value. An auction at a stamp club meeting can be just as exciting, just as much fun, and much less expensive.

If you belong to a club that does not regularly include an auction in its programs, suggest to club officers that one be initiated. It is easy to get an auction organized. Club members are invited to submit lots on which they have indicated the minimum bid they will accept. Many items are submitted without a minimum. One member of the club is selected as the auctioneer. This member usually is an extrovert, perhaps a bit of an actor, who enjoys getting up in front of a crowd, who can add some excitement to a meeting.

He or she describes the items to be offered and then begins accepting bids. When the sale is completed the buyer pays the agreed price and the club extracts a small commission, paying the difference to the seller.

There are many variations to club auctions. For instance, the auctioneer may want to start with a ridiculously high price and then begin working downward. The sale is consummated when one of the members says "Stop." The longer you wait, the lower the price. But, of course, there is a risk of some other member saying "stop" before you do, thereby denying you the chance to buy that particular item.

Another variation of club auctions is to put the items to be sold in shoe or cigar boxes and pass them among the members. Each member who wants to bid writes his or her name on a slip of paper and drops it in the box, which then is passed to the next member. This member, without looking at earlier bids, adds his or her offer. Those who do not want to bid on a particular lot simply pass the box to the next member.

When all have had a chance to bid, the boxes are returned to the auctioneer, who sorts the bid slips. Interest can be added to an auction of this type—and returns increased—by substituting a system of penalties and rewards. The highest bidder gets to buy the item. The lowest bidder is penalized a token amount and the second highest bidder is given this amount. This keeps out bids that are too low and it adds interest by seeing how close you can come to the correct bid without actually buying the item.

In a club in which there are both youngsters and older collectors, there is an obligation on the auctioneer to protect the neophytes when possible. Thus, an auctioneer who sees a youngster bidding two dollars on an item that normally sells for about seventy-five cents should at least caution the bidder that the item is available at a lower price through regular retail channels. Such action sometimes will irritate the avaricious, who might want to make a "killing" by selling inferior material at high prices to the uninformed. But a club that builds a reputation for caring about its auction bidders will soon develop a credibility that will pay dividends in the long run.

Auction sales are not final until the customer is satisfied with the stamps purchases—whether the auction takes place on the floor of an auction house, by mail, or at a local stamp club. Any lot found to be other than as described must be the basis for cancellation of the offer.

Once you get into the fun of auctions, you probably will want to submit items of your own for sale. There are some things you should know about presenting your lots in ways that will invite the highest bids. Packaging is a major step. An attractive presentation will draw attention and increase the number of potential bidders. If you put the stamps in plastic bags, arrange them so that the potential buyers can see both the back and the front of the stamp. Group like items together. A lot made up of stamps showing flowers, for instance, is much more likely to attract bidders than one that is made up just of a batch of unsorted stamps—although the unsorted lot may include more valuable items.

Write a careful description of what you have for sale, and stress any unusual features. This helps both the potential buyers and the auctioneer. A collection of covers becomes more interesting if the auctioneer is able to point out that all the covers have unusual commercial markings, cachets, or some other feature.

Be honest in your description. If the stamp is missing a corner perforation, say so instead of hoping this defect will go unnoticed. If you are preparing a packet of worldwide stamps, don't put only the flashy items in the front and then load the back of the envelope with common, less desirable stamps. Sure, put the bright stamps in the front, but also put some of the others up there too, so the buyer has a better idea of what the envelope contains.

Be specific in your descriptions. Are the stamps mint, never hinged, all different, all from one country, all from Iron Curtain countries? Such information is of interest to the buyer, and it should be provided by the seller.

Auctions are a fun way to buy stamps. They also often provide opportunities to find real bargains. Investigate them as part of your process of growing into an experienced collector.

10

Collecting Blocks

Saving blocks of stamps has been part of stamp collecting for many years. In the United States, this usually involves the collecting of unused stamps, but there are some collectors of used blocks.

The blocks to be collected come in many varieties. There are plate blocks, ZIP blocks, Mail Early blocks, Copyright blocks, and just plain blocks of four. In recent years, the United States has issued many stamps where four or more designs are covered on a single pane, thus making it possible to collect four different stamps that combine to form a block. In fact, the value of stamps issued in this way is diminished when the block is broken up and the pattern created by the stamps is destroyed.

Perhaps the most popular form of block collecting is that which deals with plate blocks of U.S. issues. For many years, the United States has used one or more numbers on each pane of stamps. This was an identifying mark for the printers and had nothing to do with the value of the stamp.

Collectors ordinarily save the four stamps forming a block closest to the plate number, including the plate number in the selvage, or scrap paper, found at the edge of a pane of stamps. In some earlier U.S. issues the plate numbers were placed farther up the edge of the sheet, necessitating the collecting of six stamps with the number adjacent to the middle two in order to have a plate block. As the number of colors used in stamp production increased, the number of plate numbers assigned to a single pane also increased. This made it necessary to have eight, ten, or more stamps to complete

SIX STAMPS were required for a plate block of this type, with the plate number positioned in the middle of the block.

the block, depending on the number of plate numbers. Where multiple plate numbers are used, collectors usually collect the two rows of stamps nearest the plate numbers.

A "pane" of stamps is one fourth of a sheet. Plate numbers appear in the selvage at the corners of the sheet. On a stamp that has one plate number, there might be two hundred stamps on the sheet (fifty on each pane) and the plate number would appear on each pane. It would be at the lower left on one pane; the upper left on another; the upper right on a third; and the lower right on the fourth.

THIS BLOCK has five plate numbers. Two rows adjacent to the plate numbers are collected to form the plate block. Since it was necessary to destroy one of the blocks of four in the design pattern to form the block, a plate block of this type is more expensive.

PLATE BLOCK of four of a definitive stamp having a single plate number.

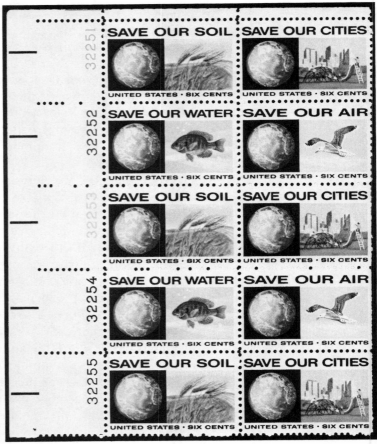

Some collectors try to get what are called "matched sets," that is, the same plate number on blocks from all four positions. Since more than one plate number will be assigned to a printing, this could mean the need to collect four, eight, or twelve or more blocks, depending on the size of the printing. The problem gets even more complex when you are dealing with multicolor printings in which there are two or more plate numbers per pane.

Another complexity was inadvertently introduced into collecting matched sets when the United States issued the John Paul Jones stamp in 1979. This was the first commemorative U.S. stamp to be printed by a commercial firm as part of an experiment to cut stamp production costs. The firm doing the printing used a wrong-sized replacement for a worn-out perforating wheel. As a result, about 30 percent of the stamps are perforated 12 x 12; about 40 percent are perforated 11 x 12, and the rest are perforated 11 x 11.

Two sets of printing cylinders were used to provide the five-color stamps. The plate numbers were about evenly divided. The plate numbers in this particular series of stamps are specially designed to identify non-government printing, and therefore do not follow the usual sequence. The numbers are preceded by the letter "A" and run in sequence from A0001 to A0010.

The 12 x 12 perforation variety appears on panes bearing plate numbers A0001 through A0005 only. The 11 x 11 variety appears only on panes bearing plate numbers A0006 through A0010. The 11 x 12 variety appears on panes bearing plate numbers from both sets. What all this means to you as a collector is that you will have three different spaces in your album for this stamp. Additionally, if you want to collect matched sets of blocks you will have to have not only the usual concerns for the right numbers and the right position, but will also have to check the perforations.

Plate-block collecting obviously is getting more complicated, and this complexity is causing a gradual drop in the number of plate-block collectors. Some complain that the varying number of stamps needed to make a plate block creates difficulty in providing attractive mountings, since the size of the blocks vary. Others are concerned with the price, which in some instances rises sharply when you have to buy as many as twenty stamps to get a plate block.

Still another complication is that there is no equal distribution of the number of sheets of stamps printed from a single plate. Therefore, a plate number might appear on only a small part of the press run before the number is retired because of damage or some other reason. The sheets produced from such "short-run" plates would obviously carry blocks that would be scarcer than others and thus command a higher price.

One result of the disenchantment with plate-block collecting has been a shift to interest in blocks of other types.

One such variety had an interesting but short life span. It was the collecting of "Mail Early" blocks. These blocks are so identified because the "Mail Early" legend appears in the selvage at the edge of the panes. It appeared on commemorative stamps in 1968 and continued until 1979, when it had to be dropped to make room for the copyright notice that now must appear on panes of all U.S. stamps. The "Mail Early" inscription appeared on some definitive stamps in the 1965–68 Prominent American series.

"MAIL EARLY" block of four with the mail-early inscription at the lower right. If a block of six were collected, the inscription would be adjacent to the center stamp in the outside row.

There are no extremely valuable blocks in the series, although some have premium prices because of unusual circumstances. For instance, the six-cent Franklin Roosevelt definitive, issued in January 1966, carries a premium on "Mail Early" blocks since there were several printings of this issue and not all of them carried the "Mail Early" inscription.

The "Mail Early" blocks of the 1965–78 period were interesting and attractive. They carried the inscriptions in such a position that it was possible to get a block of six stamps with the slogan aligned with the middle row. This proved to be short lived, as the United States moved more and more into multicolor stamps, which meant it was necessary to destroy a plate or ZIP block in order to get a block of six including the "Mail Early" inscription. This caused collectors to switch to collecting "Mail Early" with a block of four stamps instead of six.

Collecting of blocks was further complicated by the switch in size of U.S. commemoratives to a number of jumbo-sized varieties, some in horizontal and some in vertical formats. This made the handling of both plate blocks and "Mail Early" blocks unwieldy, created problems in trying to find suitable albums, and made it necessary to buy a wide variety of mounts.

The collecting of "Mail Early" blocks will never be widespread, since they are no longer issued. The collecting of plate blocks will probably give way to other types of collecting since many collectors consider the trouble and cost involved no longer worth the effort.

One approach that seems to be gaining in popularity is the collecting of plate-number singles: that is, collecting a single stamp with a plate number on it. It is important to remember that in this type of collecting the selvage must be left attached at the bottom and the side of the stamp in the case of panes with single plate numbers. On panes having multiple plate numbers, no set pattern has been established.

ZIP blocks are still being produced and they have a small following. These blocks consist of the four U.S. stamps nearest the margin where the "Mr. ZIP" inscription appears. ZIPs are of special interest because varied designs are used in the logotype in the inscription. Sometimes Mr. ZIP is portrayed as looking at you; other times he is shown running. Since ZIP codes are here to stay—and, in fact, will soon be expanding to nine digits—the Mr. ZIP imprints are likely to be around for some time. ZIP imprints are positioned across the pane from the plate block, and thus do not conflict with the plate block when they are removed from the pane.

"MR. ZIP" block, with the figure in the upper left corner. Sometimes "Mr. Zip" is shown as a running figure.

Many collectors of ZIP blocks prefer to create their own album pages, using blank pages and drawing boxes of appropriate size around the blocks. The size of the box, of course, will vary, depending on whether the stamps are standard or jumbo sized, and whether they are definitives or commemoratives.

Pricewise the "Mail Early" and ZIP blocks follow the trend of the stamp to which they are attached, and there are no especially valuable blocks in either category. Both "Mr. ZIP" and "Mail Early" blocks generally sell for less than plate blocks.

The "Mail Early" blocks that command premium prices usually are those pulled from panes where multiple stamp designs appear on the same pane. To get a "Mail Early" block of six it is necessary to separate one of the blocks containing the four different designs. Since the blocks are worth more when they are left intact, separating them to get a "Mail Early" block means the "Mail Early" block would be more expensive than one taken from a pane of stamps having only one design.

This was particularly true in the case of the Christmas stamps of 1970, which featured four different early toys on four different stamps on the same pane. Those stamps already are fairly expensive in plate-block and regular block form, and the fact that one such block had to be destroyed to create the "Mail Early" block of six makes such "Mail Early" blocks both scarce and expensive.

This particular set of stamps provides further complications in that it was issued generally in regular form but also in pre-cancelled form in an experiment with precancelling of Christmas stamps to speed mail processing—thus creating additional varieties.

Should you go into block collecting? That is a matter of personal choice. Some collectors simply add a few blocks to their collections of singles. Others go all out for blocks and ignore the single stamps. The die-hard collectors use albums especially designed for plate blocks and put out by a number of album companies. Because of the variations in block sizes, some collectors elect to use blank pages and add their own ornamentation. Some collect used blocks. These are harder to come by but less expensive to collect.

United Nations stamps have marginal inscriptions on each pane, creating a specialized area of collecting in which an effort is made to get blocks that carry the inscriptions.

Israel uses a design in the selvage, which is left attached to the stamp it adjoins. This is known as a "tab," and Israeli stamps with such tabs sell at a premium.

Many other countries use the selvage area on each pane to carry various kinds of information. Some of them run numbers across the bottom, making it easier for postal clerks to divide the panes and compute the charges when selling stamps at the post offices.

If you get into block collecting, be alert at club auctions and when visiting stamp dealers. Plate blocks generally sell very slowly and dealers sometimes are willing to let you buy an accumulation of blocks at only slightly over face value. This is particularly true of U.S. commemorative issues that have appeared since about 1950. At auctions, particularly smaller ones, you may be the only one interested in plate blocks; therefore you have a chance to pick up a bargain.

The best friend a plate-block collector can have is a postal clerk. Many clerks simply tear up the panes as stamps are sold and many plate blocks are destroyed in this fashion. But whenever a new stamp comes out, ask the postal clerk to sell you a plate block. On the current commemoratives they are often willing to do so since they sell many of the stamps over the counter and most customers merely tear off the selvage if they are sold a stamp to which the plate number is attached.

Talking with the postal clerks is a particularly good way to get plate blocks of the definitive issues. These are harder to get, since a customer asking for a stamp normally is sold a commemorative rather than a definitive. Get in the habit of asking the clerks if they have any plate blocks of the definitives, particularly of the higher denominations. You will have to contend with the fact that many postal clerks are stamp collectors and will buy the blocks and hold them in the hope the value will appreciate. However, many clerks are not collectors and will sell you the blocks, particularly if they get to know you.

If you ever have the opportunity to get a plate block of the one-dollar, two-dollar, or five-dollar stamps, jump at the chance. There is only one plate number on each pane of these varieties and there are one hundred stamps per pane. You can imagine how long it will take a small post office to sell a hundred of the one-dollar stamps, much less the two- or five-dollar varieties.

If your travels take you to small towns, try asking the postal clerks if they have any plate blocks of the older issues. When a new definitive is issued the remainders of the early varieties usually disappear very rapidly. But some remote post offices may have a couple of the panes in the drawer and will just not bother to exchange them for the newer types. Some very good stamp finds are made in remote post offices visited on vacation or business trips.

11

Stamp Shows

Almost every week you will see advertisements of stamp shows of one kind or another in the philatelic press and in the stamp columns of your local newspaper. They provide an excellent opportunity to expand your collecting interests and to add stamps and other philatelic items to your collection.

Many of the smaller stamp shows are nothing more than *bourses*, collections of dealers offering philatelic wares. The major stamp shows charge admission. The local ones usually do not.

There is an art to attending a stamp show. It begins with walking in with your hands in your pockets and keeping them there until you have walked through the exhibit and dealer areas a few times.

Visit a stamp show as you would visit a strange city. Take the complete tour first, making notes of the exhibits you want to come back to and look at in greater detail later. Glance at the various specialty items offered by each dealer and make notes of the ones that are of more than passing interest. Look especially for dealers who handle items of particular interest to you, such as plate blocks, first-day covers, postal stationery, revenue items, and the like. Most dealers will have some of each item, but only the specialists will have a wide range of items in your area of specialization.

Dealers pay a rental fee for the space they have at stamp shows. They must recoup this investment before they begin to make a profit. The dealer with the largest number of tables has made the biggest investment and therefore is likely to charge more than the small dealer with a single table.

The two best times to visit a stamp show are the first and last days. Early on the first day you can look around before the late sleepers arrive. This gives you first crack at the one-of-a-kind items. The dealers are not too busy at this point and they are usually happy to have you sit and chat while they wait for buyers. Just having you there makes them look busy and this often draws other customers.

The last day is good because it is a chance to pick up bargains. Some stamp writers contend that dealers will not bargain with you. This may be idealistically true, but it is not reality. A dealer who has had a slow show and is getting ready to pack up his stock and go back to a distant city will frequently be willing to "negotiate" if you are willing to make a reasonable offer. The best way to find out is to make an offer and see what happens. The worst you can get is a refusal.

Talk to as many dealers as you can about your collecting interests. Tell them your special needs and ask what they have to offer that would fit your collection and your budget. If you like the dealer and the prices, leave your name and address and ask the dealer to get in touch with you whenever he or she has items that fit your collection. Dealers are always buying collections and they never know from one week to the next what specialty items will turn up.

At the bigger shows—these usually occur in the major cities in the spring and fall of the year—you are likely to find postal substations—offering special cancellations as well as current mint issues at face value. The post office departments of the United States, the United Nations, Great Britain, and Canada frequently have displays at major shows in the United States. It is often possible to get on the mailing lists of the countries represented; this will bring you advance news of new issues. The covers in which these news releases are mailed often carry the stamps of the issuing country and are in themselves collectors' items.

Sometimes the United States or the United Nations will plan a first-day ceremony as part of the show proceedings. This makes it possible to get first-day cancellations not only on covers but on a wide variety of other items such as programs, admission tickets, souvenir cards, and the like. The first-day ceremony usually includes the presence of the stamp designer and postal officials. It is often possible to get those people to autograph your program or covers, thus adding to the interest and the value of the item.

The major show also generally has a scheduled series of lectures and special presentations at various times. This gives you a chance to hear speakers with specialized knowledge of their subjects.

The major stamp societies also often offer presentations about their organizations and may present programs dealing with such topics as insuring a stamp collection. They also have experts present who can help you identify stamps and tell you whether or not they are genuine.

While the big stamp shows offer more exhibits and a wider range of dealers, the smaller shows often are more fun to attend. Such shows generally include local dealers who are anxious to get to know collectors in the area. The dealers pay less for the tables, and therefore are not as concerned with fast sales to buyers of high-priced material. The smaller shows, of course, draw smaller crowds, giving the dealers more time to chat with collectors. Further, the dealers are much more likely to be interested in having you return as a regular customer than they are in making a quick killing on a single sale.

You are more likely to find bargains at smaller shows than at the major exhibits. The dealers are frequently part-timers and often lack the time and the expertise to fully research the philatelic oddities that come across their counters. For instance, a dealer who buys a foreign collection often strips out the most immediately resalable items and puts the rest up for sale at a few cents per stamp. Knowledgeable collectors go through such collections and spot things like special cancellations, stamps placed incorrectly in the album, and other differences that take the stamps out of the "few cents" category and make them worth much more. This aspect of collecting is discussed in greater detail in chapter 2.

Small shows often offer cachets that are prepared by a local group. While not of particular philatelic value, covers carrying such cachets make good conversation pieces when you display your collection.

Sample copies of philatelic publications are often available free, even at the smaller shows. At a major show special "show prices" are frequently offered to attract new subscribers.

As your collecting advances you may want to take part in a stamp show as an exhibitor instead of as just a visitor. The opportunities are wide open, particularly in the smaller shows.

Let's look at how you might go about getting your stamp club interested in sponsoring a show and the part you might play in it.

If you are in an active club that has about a dozen members, you have the basis for putting on a stamp show that will not only provide members with an opportunity to display their collections, but will serve as a good way to get publicity for the club and thereby attract new members.

A first step is getting all of the members actively involved. Some will want to prepare exhibits, others will volunteer to help set up the show, handle the publicity, arrange for the judges, and take care of the myriad other details that go into a successful show.

Select a date which will not conflict with other local events. Avoid weekends like July 4 or Labor Day, when there are too many other activities competing for the available time. Pick a site large enough to house the displays but not so large as to make visitors feel lost as they move from one exhibit to the next. Some clubs elect to have their shows in the local library or community center. Check ahead of time to see if the site selected will allow for the sale of stamps during the show. While having a few dealers present is a good way to help pay the bills and attract the crowds, many places such as libraries do not allow commercial sales on the premises. A church basement or a donated meeting hall could solve this problem.

Decide on the size of the show in advance. Do this by determining how many collectors are likely to exhibit, and the size of the presentations they are prepared to make. An exhibit can be made up of many pages or it can consist of a single sheet.

It is a good idea to group the exhibits into categories so beginners don't have to compete against advanced collectors. If there are too many exhibits, it may be practical to break them down further into groups such as topical collections, U.S. collections, worldwide collections, specialty items, and any other suitable categories.

Awards are an essential part of a stamp show. In the smaller shows these consist of ribbons, which can be purchased at minimal cost out of the club treasury. Generally a blue ribbon is given for first place, a red ribbon for second, and a white ribbon for third.

Judges can be club members who are not exhibiting, or they can be stamp writers or collectors from outside the club. Once the exhibits are received at the club they should be numbered and marked for the areas in which they are to be displayed. The name of the collector should not be identified since you want to make it possible to have impartial judging. The judging generally takes place before the show opens to the public, with the winners announced during the show and the appropriate ribbons affixed to their entries. At the larger shows, tropies are often substituted for the ribbons.

You don't have to be an advanced collector to enter an exhibit at a small-club show, nor do you have to invest a large amount of money in your display. At such shows, judges generally are concerned with the amount of effort and ingenuity you put into preparing your display.

It is important here to separate a stamp show display from a competitive exhibit. There are virtually no limits on what can be put into a display. Competitive exhibits, on the other hand, must conform to strict rules as to what may be entered and how it must be presented.

A display can be enhanced by the addition of interesting non-philatelic material dealing with the same subject. A display of Boy or Girl Scouts on stamps, for instance, might include merit badges, handbooks, and even photographs along with the stamps. A competitive exhibit on the same subject would be limited to philatelic material that has a postal relationship to the subject of the entry.

The obvious place for the neophyte exhibitor to begin is in a presentation by the local stamp club. The items to be shown should be mounted on blank pages. There should be descriptive material so that visitors to the show can readily understand what is being displayed.

Any stamp catalog will provide the basic information on why a stamp was issued, the number of stamps that were printed, the date and place of issue, and any known deviations from the normal pattern, such as the existence of the stamp with color or perforation errors.

Stamps to be displayed should be under a protective cover. At the major shows, exhibits are displayed under glass. This is protection against both damage and theft. At the smaller shows a plastic-covered page is an acceptable substitute.

The first time a club attempts an exhibit or show, it should plan a limited venture and use it as a kind of philatelic research that will reveal the problems likely to be encountered when a more ambitious venture is attempted the next time.

If dealers are invited to participate, they should be charged a nominal fee for table space. If they can make some money at the first show, they are more likely to want to come back to future shows.

If the show is likely to attract a large crowd, you might want to consider having a cachet. This cachet can be designed by a club member and reproduced by your local quick-copy shop on your envelopes for a small fee. If you undertake a venture of this type, the safest approach is to take orders in advance and then print only a few more envelopes than you are sure you can sell. The remainders can be saved for door prizes at future meetings, or for use as gifts to new members.

Stamp shows, like so many other "fringe" benefits of stamp collecting, contribute to the increased enjoyment you get from your hobby when you share it with others.

12

Postal Cards

The collecting of U.S. postal cards has been a specialized part of philately for years. It is growing in popularity now as more and more collectors are using a least a few postal cards to enrich their collections. It is important to note here the difference between *postal cards*, which are the cards issued by the Postal Service and are stamped, and *postcards* which are issued by commercial firms and to which stamps must be affixed. Postcards generally are of the picture variety cherished by tourists as carriers of the most overused phrase in the English language—"Wish you were here."

The popularity of postal cards among U.S. collectors is attested to by the growth of specialized groups such as the United Postal Stationery Society, which offers its members a specialized journal and has produced a number of authoritative catalogs together with other supplementary material.

To give you an idea of the size of the challenge in collecting postal cards, there now are hundreds of U.S. varieties and the number is increasing steadily as the United States turns to using commemorative postal cards to satisfy some of the demands of groups requesting commemorative stamp issues. The number of commemorative stamps that can be issued each year is very limited; therefore the release of commemorative postal cards gets the Postal Service off the hook while at the same time satisfying collectors.

The identification of postal cards, particularly the early issues, is not as easy as it might seem at first glance. Many of

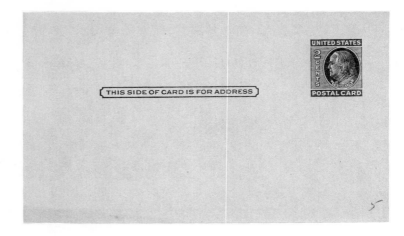

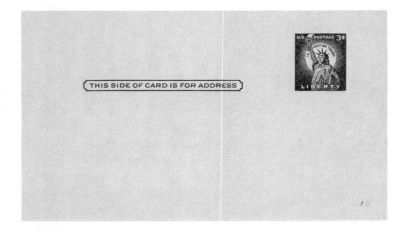

the early issues were printed on both rotary and flatbed presses. Since rotary printing involves the use of a curved plate, the stamp image tends to be stretched slightly in the direction of the curvature of the cylinder. Each variety carries a separate catalog number and goes in a separate place in your album. On some of the cards the differences are so minute it takes an expert to spot them.

Further variations occur because of differences in color, thickness, and texture of the paper used in printing the cards.

The United States had a paper shortage in 1972, and this forced the Government Printing Office to use at least two different grades of paper for cards produced that year. Both cards are white, but one is on a paper of considerably coarser texture than the other. In 1974, the printing office changed suppliers and the result was a shift to a "blue white" paper.

Many of the postal cards were printed in black ink. However, many shades of black developed during the printing process, due to the variations in the amount of ink applied.

There are even three postal cards that have watermarks. These are very early issues and the watermarks usually can be detected by holding the cards up to a strong light.

Since this book is designed primarily to introduce you to the various options open to collectors, there is no need to go into minute detail about the many varieties of postal cards, other than to make you aware that such variations exist. If you want to go deeper into the subject, your local stamp dealer, stamp club or library can refer you to appropriate supplemental material.

Single-color postal cards are printed on paper in roll form, with eighty impressions on a cylinder. Cards then are cut into sheets of forty cards and may be sold to printers in that form for the application of commercial messages.

Starting in 1956, the multicolored cards have been printed on sheet-fed lithographic presses. The number of cards per sheet varies depending on the degree of accuracy required to bring the colors into proper alignment.

There are "errors" and variations in postal cards just as there are in stamps. Occasionally cards slip through on which two or more impressions appear. This can happen if the card sheet is not removed from the press or is inserted twice, creating two impressions. Often the impressions are very close or overlap. Other times they produce a "fuzzy" appearance as one stamp is printed slightly away from the other impression.

Cards produced on rotary presses also come up with double impressions once in a while. This occurs when the press is stopped and restarted, producing a double impression. These "double prints" are listed as separate varieties in the catalogs.

Fluorescent postal-card paper has been used for more than a decade as the Postal Service moves further into automated sorting of mail. Some of the cards were printed on this type of paper intentionally, others by accident, as in 1972, when paper ran short and the printing office used whatever was available.

Collectors interested in identifying and separating the "tagged" material (a term used to identify stamps or other postal items with fluorescent coating) can do so by placing it under an ultraviolet lamp. The tagged varieties will glow.

Considerable interest is added to postal-card collecting when you include unusual cancellations and other postal markings. A few of the possibilities in this area include: flag cancels (in which the cancellation is in the shape of a flag); cancellations prepared especially for a stamp exhibition; first-day cancellations; ship cancellations; and cancellations from military post offices.

In the early days, cancellations were often applied by hand devices, providing an opportunity for postmasters to use their imagination and ingenuity. The result was a number of geometric patterns, fancy designs, and even heavy black blots. Most of the cancellations were in black, but cards are often found with cancellations in color—they are the scarcer and more valuable varieties.

In looking at an accumulation of early postal cards you are likely to find some that carry commercial messages on them. These add interest to a collection since many of the products offered no longer exist.

In addition to domestic postal cards, the United States produces cards for use on international mail. The first such card was issued in December 1879.

Beginning in 1892, the United States also produced reply cards for domestic use. This involved two cards that were issued as a single unit. The recipient got the message on the first card and used the second card to forward the reply.

The first multicolored U.S. postal card was issued in 1956 to honor the Fifth International Philatelic Exhibition, held in Washington, D.C. It was a two-cent card with a triangular shaped stamp. Overprinted "Fifth International Philatelic Exhibition," the stamp was printed in red and dark violet-blue on buff. There is a variety of this card in which the violet-blue overprint was inadvertently omitted—making the card worth many times more than the correct version.

Later in l956, the first multicolored card for international

FIRST-DAY CARDS, like first-day envelopes, increase in value if they have a cachet. Here are examples of the 1965 census card, with and without cachet.

FOREIGN NATIONS ALSO use reply cards. Here is an example of an early Canadian variety.

REPLY CARDS are designed to provide the recipient with an easy way to respond. Shown are the two parts of the 1967 card promoting tourism.

"TOURISM YEAR OF THE AMERICAS" (1972) saw the release of three 6-cent cards (described in the chapter on postal cards) and two airmail cards. The fronts of the regular issues and the backs of the airmails are shown.

use was released. It was a four-center showing the Statue of Liberty and was printed in red and blue on buff.

One set of cards that proved popular with collectors was the "Tourism Year of the Americas," released in 1972. It was made up of three cards, each with a six-cent stamp embossed on the front and four illustrations on the back. The stamp on the first card featured the U.S. frigate *Constitution*. The pictures on the back showed Yosemite, Mount Rushmore, Niagara Falls, and Williamsburg.

The second card spotlighted Monument Valley on the stamp and the reverse featured Monterey, Redwoods, Gloucester, and U.S.S. *Constitution*.

The third card showed the Gloucester Lighthouse. The reverse depicted a rodeo, a Mississippi riverboat, the Grand Canyon, and Monument Valley.

There have been many colorful issues over the last dozen years. Some of the more striking have included the six-cent issue saluting the International Boy Scout Jamboree, which was held in Idaho in 1967.

More recent issues have spotlighted historic preservation and have included the 1977 nine-center featuring the Federal Court House at Galveston, Texas, and the 1978 ten-center showing the Cincinnati Music Hall. Other 1978 issues featured the U.S. Coast Guard training ship *Eagle* on a fourteen-cent card; and a ten-center showing Molly Pitcher firing the cannon at the Battle of Monmouth.

Postal cards usually are collected by saving the entire card. This is essential, particularly where you get into the more elaborate cards of recent years.

Keep in mind that condition is important in collecting cards, just as it is in collecting stamps. Cards that are worn, soiled, or damaged are worth considerably less than those in fine condition.

13

Just for Fun

Trivia quizzes are fun, whether given by an individual or as the program at a club meeting. They are especially appropriate when they focus on philatelic matters and are used as an "ice breaker" at a stamp club meeting.

Following are five quizzes with point values assigned based on the degree of difficulty. Using them as a pattern, it is easy to compile an unlimited number for use at philatelic functions.

To add interest, divide the club into groups and pit one team against the other, awarding an appropriate philatelic prize to the group with the best score.

To keep the competition fair, designate team captains and then let them pick team members in turn from those at the meeting.

QUIZ NO. 1

Five-Point Questions:

1. What is the highest denomination in the 1932 Washington Bicentennial issue?
2. Who appears on the U.S. two-cent definitive of 1965?
3. A U.S. commemorative stamp was issued on Veterans Day in 1979. It honors the veterans of what war?
4. What Polish astronomer appears on a 1973 U.S. commemorative?

Ten-Point Questions:

1. The first U.S. Champion of Liberty stamp was an eight-cent issue. It appeared in 1957. Who does it feature?
2. Who appears on the twelve-cent U.S. definitive issued in 1965?
3. Who is the Indian shown on the six-cent American Indian commemorative of 1968?

Twenty-five-Point Questions:

1. Four colonial crafts are depicted on the American Bicentennial issue of 1972. What are they?
2. What is shown on the five-dollar definitive of the U.S. 1922–25 series?

ANSWERS TO
QUIZ NO. 1

Five-Point Questions:

1. Ten cents
2. Frank Lloyd Wright
3. Vietnam
4. Nicholas Copernicus

Ten-Point Questions:

1. Philippines President Ramon Magsaysay
2. Henry Ford
3. Chief Joseph

Twenty-five-Point Questions:

1. Glass Blower
   Silversmith
   Wigmaker
   Hatter
2. The head of the Freedom Statue from the Capitol dome in Washington, D.C.

QUIZ NO. 2

Five-Point Questions:

1. The inventor of the electric light is honored on a 1929 U.S. issue. Who is he?
2. Presidents Truman and Johnson appear on memorial stamps issued in 1973. What was the denomination on the stamps?
3. What famous hero appears on the 1979 U.S. Christmas stamp?
4. Who is featured on the one-cent stamp of the Prominent American series of 1965?

Ten-Point Questions:

1. What former U.S. President appears on a six-cent stamp issued in 1965?
2. The publisher of *The New York Times* from 1896 through 1935 appears on a thirteen-cent 1976 commemorative. Who is he?
3. A 1959 U.S. stamp pushed World Peace Through World Trade. What was the denomination?

Twenty-five-Point Questions:

1. Name three Americans who have appeared on five-dollar stamps.
2. What musical instrument is shown on the 7.9-cent bulk-mail stamp?

ANSWERS TO QUIZ NO. 2

Five-Point Questions:

1. Thomas A. Edison
2. Eight cents
3. Santa Claus
4. Thomas Jefferson

Ten-Point Questions:

1. Franklin D. Roosevelt
2. Adolph S. Ochs
3. Eight cents

Twenty-five-Point Questions:

1. Alexander Hamilton
   Calvin Coolidge
   John Bassett Moore
2. Drum

QUIZ NO. 3

Five-Point Questions:

1. A five-cent U.S. stamp of 1966 honors a man who went around planting trees. What was his name?
2. What is the highest denomination in the Columbian issue of 1893?
3. Who appears on the U.S. fifteen-cent stamp of 1965?
4. How many stamps are there in the Overrun Countries issue of 1943–44?

Ten-Point Questions:

1. A two-cent stamp of 1932 shows two people planting a tree. What event is being honored?
2. Who appears on the three-cent definitive stamp of 1965?
3. Much confusion resulted when the wrong perforating wheel was used on a 1979 U.S. commemorative. What stamp was involved?

Twenty-five-Point Questions:

1. Moina Michael appears on a three-cent stamp of 1948 in the U.S. What was her claim to fame?
2. A famous playwright appears on both the sheet and coil version of one-dollar U.S. stamps. Who is he?

QUIZ NO. 4

Five-Point Questions:

1. Who is the nurse shown on the U.S. thirteen-cent commemorative issued in 1976?
2. The United States issued only one airlift stamp. It came out in 1968. What was the denomination?
3. A U.S. stamp issued in 1978 shows a coin. What coin is it?
4. Who appears on the U.S. thirteen-cent stamp of 1965?

Ten-Point Questions:

1. The secretary general of the United Nations is shown on a famous U.S. "error stamp" of 1962. What was his name?
2. Who appears on the twenty-one-cent stamp in the U.S. definitive series?
3. What famous doctors were the subject of a five-cent U.S. commemorative in 1964?

Twenty-five-Point Questions:

1. The Wildlife Conservation series of U.S. issues of 1972 shows birds and animals. Name them.
2. Two women appear on U.S. definitives between 1965 and 1978. Name them.

ANSWERS TO QUIZ NO. 4

Five-Point Questions:

1. Clara Maass
2. One dollar
3. Indian Head Penny
4. John F. Kennedy

Ten-Point Questions:

1. Dag Hammarskjold
2. Chester A. Arthur
3. The Mayo Brothers

Twenty-five-Point Questions:

1. Fur seals
   Cardinal
   Brown pelican
   Bighorn sheep
2. Eighteen-cent Dr. Elizabeth Blackwell
   Fifty-cent Lucy Stone

QUIZ NO. 5

Five-Point Questions:

1. A 1966 U.S. five-cent stamp saluted the one-thousandth anniversary of a European nation. What country was it?
2. Who is shown on the first U.S. stamp? It was a five-cent stamp issued in 1847.
3. Who appears on the four-cent U.S. definitive of 1965?
4. Churchill Downs is the site of a sport stamp issued by the United States in 1974. What sport is honored?

Ten-Point Questions:

1. The first U.S. space stamp came out in 1948. It was a three-cent stamp showing a rocket. At what military base did the rocket firing take place?
2. Frederick Douglass appears on a stamp in the Prominent American Series of 1965. What is the denomination?
3. What famous U.S. general appears on the twenty-cent stamp issued by the U.S. in 1965?

Twenty-five-Point Questions:

1. The U.S. 1976 Bicentennial issue included a sheet of fifty state flags. The flag of what state appears in the upper left-hand corner?
2. The Winter Olympics issue of 1976 featured four sports. Name them.

ANSWERS TO QUIZ NO. 5

Five-Point Questions:

1. Poland
2. Benjamin Franklin
3. Abraham Lincoln
4. Horse racing (and the Kentucky Derby)

Ten-Point Questions:

1. Fort Bliss, El Paso, Texas
2. Twenty-five cents
3. George C. Marshall

Twenty-five-Point Questions:

1. Delaware
2. Running
   Skating
   Diving
   Skiing

14

"Back of the Book"

REVENUE STAMPS

Uncle Sam has been in the taxing business for many years. More than a century ago the government began issuing adhesive stamps to certify that the required taxes had been paid on various articles of merchandise. Today, those stamps have become an interesting addition to postage stamp collecting.

In the summer of 1862, the government began to advertise for private companies to submit bids for the printing of revenue stamps. The contracts were won by the firm of Butler and Carpenter of Philadelphia, and you will find them identified on many of the plates of revenue stamps produced during that period. The imprint reads: "Engraved by Butler & Carpenter, Philadelphia," or "Jos. R. Carpenter."

U.S. FIRST-ISSUE revenues of the Civil War era came in many varieties, including imperforate, part perforate and perforate.

There were 102 stamps in the first revenue issue. They were designed to indicate payment of tax on a specific item. The items taxed ranged from playing cards to patent medicine.

All of the revenue stamps in the first series carried a picture of George Washington and were inscribed "U.S. Internal Revenue Service," plus the use for which the stamp was intended.

These stamps often were cancelled by hand, often with the initials of the person doing the cancelling and the date. Some cancellations also were done by handstamps or even by punching the stamps. The handstamped cancelled types are generally valued higher than the pen-cancel varieties.

Collectors who save this first revenue set will find color and paper variations. Some of the set was used for as long as eight years and there were several reprintings.

This first issue, with its myriad varieties and its restricted use, created many problems for the Post Office Department. Reuse of the stamps was common, with the cancellations being washed off or otherwise removed.

When the second issue appeared in 1871, it featured new designs and made other changes. All of the stamps were printed in blue, and on a type of paper that made it more difficult to remove the cancellations.

There are only thirty stamps in the second issue. They were also marked "U.S. Internal Revenue Service," but did not further identify the specific tax to which they were related.

The new issue created more problems than it solved. The fact that all of the stamps were uniform in color confused the users and caused the issue to be abandoned after about a year. It was replaced by a third series that had different designs and was printed with varying denominations. It was used in 1871 and 1872.

Beginning in 1898, definitive stamps of 1898 were overprinted with the letters IR for "Internal Revenue." The overprints appear in a variety of type styles and sometimes appear on the stamps inverted.

DURING THE SPANISH-AMERI-CAN War era "IR" was overprinted on regular postage stamps to convert them to revenue stamps. Some came with inverted overprints. The overprinted issues were followed by two regular series of revenues picturing a contemporary battleship.

PROPRIETARY STAMPS

Whenever the nation is at war the expanded need for revenues results in the imposition of new taxes. Such was the case in 1862 when the government, responding to the financial needs created by the Civil War, passed the Revenue Act of 1862. Revenue stamps were made mandatory on boxes or packages of matches, proprietary medicines, perfume, playing cards, and many other items.

Manufacturers were permitted to have dies engraved and tax stamps printed at their own expense for application to their products. The manufacturers were willing to do so because they were given discounts to compensate for their printing costs and because the stamps carried the name of the company and thus provided additional advertising.

The tax was repealed effective July 1, 1883.

Most of the stamps were affixed to the products in a way that would cause the stamp to be destroyed when the container was opened. Stamps so damaged are less valuable than those that are not.

The stamps are found on everything from hard, brittle paper to the soft porous variety, and even on paper containing silk fibers.

MOTOR VEHICLE STAMPS

World War II brought the Motor Vehicle Use revenue stamps of 1942. These had to be attached to the windshield, and permitted the use of the vehicle for a fixed period. The design showed the price of the stamp and the period for which it was effective. This information was superimposed on the Liberty Bell, the central feature of the design. An unusual feature of these stamps is that most of them were gummed on the face—for application to windshields—and carried supplemental information on the back.

One could suppose that collecting such a stamp "on cover" would require saving the entire windshield.

The Motor Vehicle Use stamps of 1945 and 1946 carried a photo of Daniel Manning, treasury secretary under President Grover Cleveland in 1885. The stamps had gum on the face and inscriptions and control numbers on the back. Affixed to windshields, the stamps were sold with the car when the vehicles were transferred.

HUNTING STAMPS

The Migratory Bird Hunting Stamp Act has been in effect since July 1, 1934. In the thirty-seven years between then and July 1, 1971, more than 60 million hunting stamps have been sold. The revenue resulting from the sale is used primarily by the Fish and Wildlife Service to buy land for the National Wildlife Refuge System.

DUCK-HUNTING STAMP.

The stamps are about twice the size of commemorative stamps. They are sold through first- and second-class post offices. They are also available through the Philatelic Sales Branch in Washington, which generally has hunting stamps of at least the last three years available.

The first duck stamps went on sale in 1934, at one dollar each. The price rose to two dollars in 1949, to three dollars in 1959, and to five dollars beginning in 1972.

Issues before 1941 are rare, since the law required that any not issued during the year in which they applied were to be destroyed. In 1942 the rules were changed to allow the unsold stamps to be turned over to the Post Office Department for sale to collectors.

The design for each year's hunting stamp is chosen in a nationwide contest.

It is not possible, in a general type of book, to do more than touch on the many varieties of revenue or tax stamps existing not only in the United States but in many other nations.

Additionally, there are many stamps issued by states to cover sales tax and other fees. There are many varieties of documentary stamps, such as those appearing on such legal papers as stock transfers or real estate deeds. There are tax stamps for cigarettes, for narcotics, for customs fees, for alcoholic beverages, playing cards, and boats. Tax stamps have been required for cigarette tubes, canned fruit, and firearms. There are silver-tax and potato-tax stamps. The prohibition

THE DEPRESSION of the 1930s found many people rolling their own cigarettes. The tubes used for making these cigarettes were subject to a tax, and a special stamp was issued for that purpose.

WINE-TAX STAMP.

era brought us tax stamps to cover liquor which, while banned from general sale, could be made available by prescription for medicinal purposes.

There are a number of reasons why collecting "back of the book" material is a good sideline to your basic collection. First, there is no continuing flood of new issues. Second, the stamps can be "battered" and retain value. Revenue collectors generally concentrate on used varieties, since mint copies are often difficult to obtain. Most revenue stamps in the United States are still a bargain when compared with the prices of other stamps. Take heed, however, as they are catching up fast.

Foreign revenues, on the other hand, remain a bargain, as they remain undiscovered by many collectors.

It takes a bit more work to collect revenues than it does to collect other types of stamps. Not all of the issues are outlined in catalogs—particularly the foreign issues. There is no steady flow of new literature on the subject. A case in point is the Forbin Revenue Catalog of 1914, still the definitive work on revenue issues.

There are still revenue stamps on liquor bottles and on old legal papers. Periodically offices close out their files and throw out legal papers that have become outdated. These often carry the early revenue stamps. The stamps also turn up in some accumulations and in the backs of old albums sold as part of a collection. Frequently both the collector and the dealer ignore the value of the stamps when they judge a collection's value. The collector who is alert to the value of the "back of the book" stamps usually can pick up bargains by shopping around.

15

Buying and Selling Collections

It may seem strange to discuss selling your collection at a time when you are just beginning to get more deeply involved in the hobby. However, there probably will be a number of times in your collecting years when you want to dispose of all or part of your collection.

For instance, you may decide to switch from a generalized to a specialized collection; you will want to dispose of the stamps that no longer interest you and use the proceeds to buy stamps that fit your new collecting interests. You may decide to limit your collection to the stamps of a certain time period and thus will want to eliminate from the collection stamps that were issued outside that time period. You may inherit a collection with many stamps of interest to you—and others that are not. Once again, you will be faced with the prospect of selling all or part of a collection.

Before talking about the various options open to you, let's look at how a dealer approaches the appraisal of a stamp collection. The dealer can tell a great deal about your collecting habits just by spending a short time with your collection. He can tell, for instance, whether you collect mint stamps or used; whether you collect complete or short sets; whether you have certain key sets such as the Norse American issue, higher values of the Columbians, or the early airmails.

He will look at the early United States definitives and see if you have them in their proper places. By spot-checking a half-dozen issues he will know if you are a knowledgeable collector. He will know if you have checked perforations, water-

Issued in honor of famous American Authors

Issued in honor of famous American Poets

Issued in honor of famous American Educators

Issued in honor of famous American Scientists

DEALERS look at collections to see if you collect full sets or only the lower values.

marks, and the other subtle differences that make seemingly identical stamps go in different places in your album and have considerably different value. He will look to see how conscious you are of condition. If your collection includes stamps that are torn, creased, heavily cancelled, and poorly mounted, he will mentally begin reducing the amount he will offer you.

By a quick flip through your album—particularly in the case of a collection of foreign stamps, he will know how you are acquiring your stamps. If the collection represents years of accumulating stamps that were purchased in ten- or twenty-five-cent packets, this will be readily obvious. If, on the other hand, your collection includes stamps that came off mail in a family business or through connections with a commercial firm, this, too, will be obvious, since there will probably be many stamps of higher denominations.

In the case of foreign stamps, the dealer will be looking to see if the bulk of the stamps comes from popular countries that are widely collected—Great Britain, Ireland, Vatican,

France, and various non-Iron Curtain countries—and he will want to see if you have some of the high-value issues and scarcer stamps from those countries.

He will complete his estimate with an educated guess as to the total number of common stamps you have. This is often done by counting the stamps on about thirty pages and then multiplying by the number of pages that seem to have the average number of stamps on them. This is not scientific or specific, but it provides a pretty good guess for an initial estimate.

The procedure described can, of course, be reversed if you are the buyer instead of the seller. Following the same steps, you can get a good idea of how much you should offer for a collection. While we are talking here about selling collections, bear in mind that buying entire collections can be a very good way to add to your own collection. A collection acquired at a reasonable price can fill many holes in your album, and you can sell the remainders.

When you decide to sell a collection, there are several options open to you. These include sale to another collector, selling at auction, sale to a dealer, or selling outright to a wholesale house. The method you choose should be determined by what you have to sell. Let's look at some of the various sales possibilities and consider the advantages and disadvantages of each.

If you have a small collection you might want to consider selling to another collector. This assumes that you have plenty of time to sell the collection and that you enjoy haggling. Such a sale is best accomplished through your local stamp club. The collectors there will be familiar with your collection, and there will be at least some members to whom purchase of your collection would represent advancement in the hobby.

There are some disadvantages to selling under these conditions. The prospective buyers may not have ready cash. They may not want to buy the entire collection: they may have most of the stamps you have already. They may decide that you have some stamps incorrectly identified and are thus turned off on the whole collection.

If, after reviewing all of the possible pitfalls, you decide this is the way you want to go, publicize the availability of your collection as much as possible. Invite club members to look at the collection at one meeting, and then announce that it will be sold to the highest bidder at the next. Or, you may decide what you want for the collection and simply sell it to the first buyer who meets your price.

If your collection has a high percentage of better-grade or

high-catalog items, sale to an individual may not be practical, since it will be unlikely that one collector would want all of the stamps or would have the money to pay for them. Under such circumstances, you might want to consider dealing with an auction house.

The biggest disadvantage in dealing with a large auction firm is time. The stamps have to be divided into lots, priced, cataloged, and indexed. You will be charged a commission, which could go as high as 25 percent of the value of the collection. Despite all of these disadvantages, you still may find it advisable to deal with such a firm. It will reach far more potential buyers than you could as an individual. Further, it will be reaching the specialized collectors who may be particularly interested in some parts of your collection. It will take care of the collection of payments from the buyers and will send you a check. (Items not sold will be returned to you.) Auction buyers, for the most part, are bargain hunters. However, they also include specialists who often are willing to pay more than the catalog price for an item they particularly want.

Before consigning your collection to an auction house, shop around. Write to a number of the firms and ask the terms under which they will sell your collection. Find out the time frames in which they operate and when they make payment. You might also ask for any tips they have on how to prepare the material so it will realize the best possible price.

Some auction firms will buy your collection outright and then resell it. This has the advantage of giving you spot cash, but it means you probably will get less for the stamps, since the auction house has to make a profit on the resale.

If your collection is small and does not include many high-value items, you might want to consider outright sale to a stamp dealer in your area. All dealers are willing to buy if the price is right. Whether the price is right for you will depend in part on whether the dealer has potential customers for the material you have to sell. Few small dealers have large amounts of cash to tie up in collections that they may have to hold for a long time before reselling.

Talk with other collectors in your area and find out the experiences they have had in buying or selling collections. A dealer's reputation soon spreads among area clubs and you will know if you are likely to get a fair offer.

Some major stamp wholesalers, like H. E. Harris Co. of Boston, are constantly in the market for anything philatelic. In their effort to get collectors to sell to them they list six advantages. They make only one offer—there is no haggling to get the price up higher. They send a check along with their offer—giving the collector the option of returning the check and getting the collection back if the offer is not satisfactory. They do not charge for making the appraisal. They make their offer within a week of receipt of the collection and they have ample cash to cover even the largest of purchases. Collections not purchased are returned intact and prepaid.

Any collector contemplating the sale of a collection, by whatever means, should begin with a good idea of what buyers expect to get for their stamps. This is possible only if you keep an adequate system of records. Basically, this means having the stamps in catalog order by country. The catalog value, of course, is not a true indicator of value, since dealers usually sell at a percentage of catalog, and the percentage varies widely among countries. But the catalog value provides at least a beginning point for determining value.

What you paid for the stamps is not always a good guide to what you can hope to get when you sell them. If you made a bad deal originally, you cannot expect the next buyer to pay for your mistakes.

Be realistic in your expectations. Realize that used albums have virtually no value and therefore will be ignored when determining the value of your collection. The value of having the stamps in albums is that they are already sorted for easy resale; buyers will take this into consideration when making an offer.

Be aware that collections consist of more than stamps. When deciding what your collection is worth, take note of the "back of the book" material like revenues, postal stationery, cut squares, and similar items. Add something extra for first-day covers, plate blocks, souvenir sheets, and other items that enhance the value of a stamp collection. Be especially alert to errors and oddities, since they can add to the amount you should receive.

In discussing the potential sale, be sure the buyer knows that you are aware of these "extras" and takes them into account when making an offer.

Finally, if possible, get more than one offer. If two or more potential buyers come up with offers that come close to your expectations, take the best one. If the offers are far apart, see if you can find the reason for the difference and ask the lower bidders if they had noted certain items in the collection, which might cause them to bid higher.

Buying and selling collections is the lifeblood of the hobby. It is the major way in which philatelic items find their way into the market. An awareness of this exciting aspect of philately will add to your enjoyment of the hobby and will fill many spaces in your albums.

16

Directory of Specialized Groups

Once you decide to specialize, there are many organizations to which you can turn for information and advice. Additionally, they are a good way to get in touch with other collectors who share your interests.

This chapter presents a list of a sampling of the various specialty groups around the nation. They vary in size, from those with a handful of members to those with many thousands on their mailing lists. Some have journals and other publications you will find helpful.

Find the groups that look interesting and write for information about membership and services. When writing to them, always include a few stamps to cover postage. Some of the groups—particulary the smaller ones—are staffed by volunteers and do not have budgets for mailing sample copies of publications or other information.

The listing is alphabetical.

American Air Mail Society
1220 19th St. NW
Washington, DC 20036

American First Day Cover Society
400 Cold Spring Road, Gallery D-309
Rocky Hill, CT 06067

American Philatelic Society
Writers' Unit
9928 Lancaster Dr.
Sun City, AZ 85351

American Revenue Association
3840 Lealma Ave.
Claremont, CA 91711

American Society of Polar Philatelists
8700 Darlina
El Paso, TX 79925

Americana Unit
American Philatelic Society
Box 13
New Britain, CT 06050

Austria Philatelic Society of New York
1206 Racebrook Rd.
Woodbridge, CT 06525

Belgium Philatelic Society
Box 1197
Binghamton, NY 13902

Brazil Philatelic Association
170 Steeplechase Road
Devon, PA 19333

British Caribbean Philatelic
Representative
Box 35666
Houston, TX 77035

Canal Zone Study Group
60 - 27th Avenue
San Francisco, CA 94121

Channel Island Collectors
Box 579
New York, NY 10028

China Stamp Society
7207 - 13th Pl.
Takoma Park, MD 20012

Christmas Philatelic Club
10000 Harriet Ave. S.
Bloomington, MN 55420

Cinderella Stamp Club
15 Shooters Ave.
Harrow, Middlesex HA3 98Q
England

Civil Censorship Study Group
5443 Paseo
Kansas City, MO 64110

Confederate Stamp Alliance
Box 5-585
Fort Richardson, AK 99505

Costa Rica Collectors Society
Rte. 3 Box 72
Marble Falls, TX 78654

Croatian Philatelic Society
c/o Bottone, Thompson Dr.
Washingtonville, NY 10992

Czechoslovak Philatelic Society
5208 Jackson St.
Hollywood, FL 33021

Eire Philatelic Association
Box 33112
Denver, CO 80233

Empire State Postal Society
54 Ramsey Pl.
Albany, NY 12208

Europa Study Unit
1633 Florida Ave.
Johnstown, PA 15902

Falkland Islands Philatelic Society
8 Thomas St.
Springvale, ME 04083

Fire Service in Philately
Box 456
Placida, FL 33946

Flag Cancel Society
664 Chester St.
Ogden, UT 84404

France and Colonies Society
Attn: John Lievsay
245 Park Avenue, 36th Floor
New York, NY 10017

Franklin D. Roosevelt Philatelic Society
Box 150
Clinton Corners, NY 12514

Germany Philatelic Society
Box 328
Syracuse, NY 13201

Great Britain Overprints Society
60 Church Lane
Eaton, Norwich, NR4 6NY,
England

Guatemala Collectors Society
Box 246
Troy, NY 12181

Haitian Philatelic Society
2117 Oak Lodge Road
Baltimore, MD 21228

Helvetia Philatelic Society
48 Division Ave.
Summit, NJ 07901

Hungarian Philatelic Society
Box 1162
Fairfield, CT 06430

Indo-China Philatelic Society
1133 Bryce Way
Ventura, CA 93003

Japanese Philatelic Society
Box 961
State College, PA 16801

Journalists, Artists, Poets on Stamps
Box 150
Clinton Corners, NY 12514

Junior Philatelists of America
209 Runkle Hall
University Park, PA 16802

Maritime Postmark Society
141 Gordon Ave.
Wadsworth, OH 44281

Masonic Study Unit
213 W. Oakley Dr. SW Apt. 106
Westmont, IL 60559

Massachusetts Postal Research League
1040 Plymouth St.
Abingdon, MA 02351

Mesoamerican Archeology Study Unit
Box 1442
Riverside, CA 92502

Mexico-Elmhurst Philatelic Society
5825 Dorchester Ave. 10W
Chicago, IL 60637

Minnesota Postal History Society
1643 Maple Knoll
St. Paul, MN 55113

Mobile Post Office Society
4621 E. Don Jose Dr.
Tucson, AZ 85718

Netherlands Philatelic Society
Box 44-C
Holland, MI 49423

New Jersey Postal History Society
102 Woodland Road
Madison, NJ 07940

Oceania Stamp Society
Box 82643
San Diego, CA 92138

Ohio Postal History Society
2218 Jackson Blvd.
University Heights, OH 44118

Old World Archaeological Study Unit
128 Bartholdi Ave.
Jersey City, NJ 07305

Pennsylvania Postal History Society
Box 309
Darby, PA 19023

Perfins Club
Box 82
Grandview, MO 64030

Philippine Philatelic Society
Box 1936
Manila, Philippines

Pitcairn Islands Study Group
106 Gilstrap Dr.
Greenville, SC 29609

Portuguese Philatelic Society
8441 Canoga Ave.
c/o Pure Aire Corp.
Canoga Park, CA 91304

Postal History Society
14 Rockrose Pl.
Forest Hills, NY 11375

Postal History Society of Canada
15 Westgate Cres.
Downsview, Ont. M3H 1P7,
Canada

Post Mark Collectors Club
1712 - 7th Avenue
Moline, IL 61265

Precancel Stamp Society
Box 14527
Phoenix, AZ 85063

Romanian Philatelic Club
34-24 76th St.
Jackson Heights, NY 11372

Ryukyus Philatelic Society
Box 5025
Oxnard, CA 93030

St. Helena and Dependencies
106 Gilstrap Dr.
Greenville, SC 29609

Scandinavian Collectors Club
Box 22308
Memphis, TN 38122

Space Topics Study Group
2121 Maple Road
Homewood, IL 60430

Sports Philatelists International
Box 5025
Oxnard, CA 93030

Texas Postal History Society
Box 12814
Austin, TX 78711

Thai Philatelic Society
2837 Minto Dr. Apt. 2
Cincinnati, OH 45208

The Pictorial Eleven
216 S. 28th Ave.
Yakima, WA 98902

Tuvalu Philatelic Society
Box 2760
Chicago, IL 60690

United Nations Philatelists
408 S. Orange Grove Blvd.
Pasadena, CA 91105

United Postal Stationery Society
Box 615
Bloomington, IL 61701

Universal Postal Union Collectors
3021 Nute Way
San Diego, CA 92117

U.S. Cancellation Club
Box 7005
Missoula, MT 59807

U.S. Philatelic Classics Society
Box 1011
Falls Church, VA 22041

Virginia Postal History Society
6208 Long Meadow Rd.
McLean, VA 22101

War Cover Club
Box 26
Brewster, NY 10509

Western Cover Society
9877 Elmar Ave.
Oakland, CA 94603

Wisconsin Postal History Society
150 Terrace Lane
Hartland, WI 53029

Zippy Collectors Club
2021 W. 9th St.
Emporia, KA 66801

17

Postal Philatelic Outlets

Philatelic outlets have been established at many post offices in the United States. They offer a convenient place to purchase recent U.S. issues at face value. The list is arranged alphabetically by states, and alphabetically by cities within the states. It is current as of February 1980.

ALABAMA
U.S. Post Office
251 N. 24th St.
Birmingham 35203

U.S. Post Office
101 Holmes N.W.
Huntsville 35804

U.S. Post Office
250 St. Joseph
Mobile 36601

U.S. Post Office
2256 East South Blvd.
Montgomery 36104

U.S. Post Office
1313 Second Avenue
Tuscaloosa 35401

ALASKA
(No philatelic outlets)

ARIZONA
U.S. Post Office
Osborn Station
3905 N. Seventh Ave.
Phoenix 85013

ARKANSAS
U.S. Post Office
South 6th & Rogers Ave.
Fort Smith 72901

U.S. Post Office
205 East Ridge
Harrison 72601

U.S. Post Office
Reserve and Broadway
Hot Springs National Park
71901

U.S. Post Office
310 East St.
Jonesboro 72401

U.S. Post Office
600 West Capitol
Little Rock 72201

CALIFORNIA

U.S. Post Office
Downtown Station
135 East Olive St.
Burbank 91502

Main Post Office
1900 E Street
Fresno 93706

Main Post Office
313 E. Broadway
Glendale 91209

U.S. Post Office
Hillcrest Station
303 E. Hillcrest
Inglewood 90306

Main Post Office
300 Long Beach Blvd.
Long Beach 90801

Main Post Office
300 N. Los Angeles St.
Los Angeles 90012

U.S. Post Office
Terminal Annex
900 N. Alameda
Los Angeles 90052

U.S. Post Office
Village Station
11000 Wilshire Blvd.
Los Angeles 90024

U.S. Post Office
Civic Center Annex
201 - 13th St.
Oakland 94612

Main Post Office
281 E. Colorado Blvd.
Pasadena 91109

Main Post Office
2000 Royal Oaks Dr.
Sacramento 95813

U.S. Post Office
Base Line Station
1164 North E St.
San Bernardino 92410

Main Post Office
2535 Midway Dr.
San Diego 92199

Main Post Office
7th and Mission Sts.
San Francisco 94101

Main Post Office
1750 Meridian Drive
San Jose 95101

U.S. Post Office
Spurgeon Station
615 N. Bush
Santa Ana 92701

Main Post Office
4245 West Lane
Stockton 95208

Main Post Office
15701 Sherman Way
Van Nuys 91408

COLORADO

Main Post Office
201 E. Pikes Peak
Colorado Springs 80901

Main Post Office
1823 Stout St.
Denver 80202

CONNECTICUT

Main Post Office
141 Weston St.
Hartford 06101

Main Post Office
11 Silver Street
Middletown 06457

Main Post Office
141 Church St.
New Haven 06510

Main Post Office
27 Masonic St.
New London 06320

Main Post Office
421 Atlantic St.
Stamford 06904

Main Post Office
135 Grand St.
Waterbury 06701

DELAWARE
Main Post Office
55 The Plaza
Dover 19901

Main Post Office
11th & Market Sts.
Wilmington 19801

DISTRICT OF COLUMBIA
L'Enfant Plaza Philatelic Center
475 L'Enfant Plaza West SW
20260

Harriet Tubman Philatelic Center
North Capital Street and
Massachusetts Avenue
20013

Headsville Station Philatelic Center
Smithsonian Institution
20560

Philatelic Sales Branch
U.S. Postal Service
20265
(mail sales only)

FLORIDA
U.S. Post Office
824 Manatee Avenue West
Bradenton 33506

U.S. Post Office
100 South Belcher Rd.
Clearwater 33515

U.S. Post Office
1900 W. Oakland Park Blvd.
Fort Lauderdale 33310

U.S. Post Office
401 S.E. 1st Avenue
Gainesville 32601

U.S. Post Office
1801 Polk Street
Hollywood 33022

U.S. Post Office
1110 Kings Road
Jacksonville 32201

U.S. Post Office
210 N. Missouri Ave.
Lakeland 33802

U.S. Post Office
118 North Bay Drive
Largo 33540

U.S. Post Office
2200 NW 72nd Ave.
Miami 33101

U.S. Post Office
1200 Goodlette Road N.
Naples 33940

U.S. Post Office
46 East Robinson St.
Orlando 32801

U.S. Post Office
1400 West Jordan St.
Pensacola 32501

U.S. Post Office
3135 First Avenue N.
St. Petersburg 33730

U.S. Post Office
1661 Ringland Blvd.
Sarasota 33578

U.S. Post Office
5201 Spruce St.
Tampa 33602

U.S. Post Office
801 Clematis St.
West Palm Beach 33401

GEORGIA
U.S. Post Office
1501 South Slappey Blvd.
Albany 31706

U.S. Post Office
115 Hancock Ave.
Athens 30601

U.S. Post Office
Downtown Station
101 Marietta St.
Atlanta 30304

U.S. Post Office
Downtown Station
120 - 12th St.
Columbus 31902

U.S. Post Office
364 Green St.
Gainesville 30501

U.S. Post Office
451 College St.
Macon 31201

U.S. Post Office
2 North Fahm St.
Savannah 31401

HAWAII
Main Post Office
3600 Aolele St.
Honolulu 96819

IDAHO
(No philatelic outlets)

ILLINOIS
Main Post Office
909 W. Euclid Avenue.
Arlington Heights 60004

Main Post Office
433 West Van Buren St.
Chicago 60607

U.S. Post Office
Loop Station
211 South Clark St.
Chicago 60604

Main Post Office
1000 East Oakton
Des Plaines 60018

Main Post Office
150 N. Scott Ave.
Joliet 60431

Main Post Office
123 Indianwood
Park Forest 60466

Main Post Office
211 - 19th St.
Rock Island 61201

U.S. Post Office
Edison Square Station
Waukegan 60085

INDIANA
Main Post Office
North Park Branch
44923 - 1st Ave.
Evansville 47710

Main Post Office
1300 South Harrison
Fort Wayne 46802

Main Post Office
5530 Sohl St.
Hammond 46320

Main Post Office
125 W. South St.
Indianapolis 46206

Main Post Office
3450 State Road 26, E
Lafayette 47901

Main Post Office
424 South Michigan
South Bend 46624

IOWA
Main Post Office
615 Sixth Avenue
Cedar Rapids 52401

Main Post Office
1165 Second Ave.
Des Moines 50318

Main Post Office
320 Sixth St.
Sioux City 51101

KANSAS
Main Post Office
1021 Pacific
Kansas City 66110

Main Post Office
434 Kansas Ave.
Topeka 66603

U.S. Post Office
Downtown Station
401 N. Market
Wichita 67202

KENTUCKY
Main Post Office
1088 Nadino Blvd.
Lexington 40511

U.S. Post Office
St. Mathews Station
Shelbyville Plaza
4600 Shelbyville Rd.
Louisville 40207

LOUISIANA

U.S. Post Office
750 Florida St.
Baton Rogue 70821

Main Post Office
705 Jefferson
Lafayette 70501

U.S. Post Office
3301 - 17th St.
Metairie 70004

U.S. Post Office
501 Sterlington Rd.
Monroe 71201

U.S. Post Office
701 Loyola Ave.
New Orleans 70113

U.S. Post Office
2400 Texas Ave.
Shreveport 71102

MAINE

Main Post Office
40 Western Ave.
Augusta 04330

Main Post Office
202 Harlow St.
Bangor 04401

Main Post Office
125 Forest Avenue
Portland 04101

MARYLAND

Main Post Office
900 E. Fayette St.
Baltimore 21233

Main Post Office
201 East Patrick St.
Frederick 21701

Main Post Office
6411 Baltimore Ave.
Riverdale 20840

Main Post Office
U.S. Route 50 & Naylor Rd.
Salisbury 21801

MASSACHUSETTS

Main Post Office
Post Office and Courthouse
Building
Boston 02109

Main Post Office
7 Bedford St.
Burlington 01803

Main Post Office
330 Cocituate Rd.
Framingham 01701

Main Post Office
385 Main St.
Hyannis 02601

Main Post Office
212 Fenn St.
Pittsfield 01201

Main Post Office
Long Pond Road
Plymouth 02360

U.S. Post Office
Quincy Branch
47 Washington St.
Quincy 02169

Main Post Office
2 Margin St.
Salem 01970

Main Post Office
74 Elm St.
West Springfield 01089

Main Post Office
4 East Central St.
Worcester 01603

MICHIGAN

Main Post Office
2075 W. Stadium Blvd.
Ann Arbor 48106

Main Post Office
1401 West Fort St.
Detroit 48233

Main Post Office
250 East Boulevard Dr.
Flint 48502

Main Post Office
225 Michigan Ave.
Grand Rapids 49501

Main Post Office
200 South Otsego
Jackson 49201

U.S. Post Office
Downtown Station
315 West Allegan
Lansing 48901

Main Post Office
200 West 2nd St.
Royal Oak 48068

MINNESOTA
Main Post Office
2800 West Michigan
Duluth 55806

Main Post Office
1st and Marquette Ave.
Minneapolis 55401

The Pioneer Postal Emporium
133 Endicott Arcade
St. Paul 55101

MISSISSIPPI
U.S. Post Office
Highway 49 North
Gulfport 39501

U.S. Post Office
245 East Capitol
Jackson 39205

U.S. Post Office
500 West Miln St.
Tupelo 38801

MISSOURI
Main Post Office
315 Pershing Rd.
Kansas City 64108

Northwest Plaza Station
500 Northwest Plaza
St. Ann 63074

Main Post Office
8th and Edmond
St. Joseph 64501

U.S. Post Office
Clayton Branch
7750 Maryland
St. Louis 63105

MONTANA
Main Post Office
841 South 26th
Billings 59100

NEBRASKA
Main Post Office
700 R Street
Lincoln 68501

Main Post Office
1124 Pacific
Omaha 68108

NEVADA
Main Post Office
1001 Circus Dr.
Las Vegas 89114

NEW HAMPSHIRE
Main Post Office
South Main St.
Hanover 03755

Main Post Office
955 Goffs Falls Rd.
Manchester 03103

NEW JERSEY
Main Post Office
1701 Pacific Ave.
Atlantic City 08401

Main Post Office
3 Miln Street
Cranford 07016

U.S. Post Office
Bellmawr Branch
Haag Ave. & Benigno Blvd.
Gloucester City 08030

Main Post Office
Route 35 & Hazlet 07730

Main Post Office
150 Ridgedale
Morristown 07960

Main Post Office
Federal Square
Newark 07102

Main Post Office
86 Bayard St.
New Brunswick 08901

Main Post Office
332 Ramapo Valley Rd.
Oakland 07436

Main Post Office
194 Ward St.
Paterson 07510

Main Post Office
171 Broad St.
Red Bank 07701

Main Post Office
076 Huyler St.
South Hackensack 07606

Main Post Office
680 Highway #130
Trenton 08650

Main Post Office
155 Clinton Road
West Caldwell 07006

NEW MEXICO
Main Post Office
1135 Broadway N.E.
Albuquerque 87101

NEW YORK
Main Post Office
445 Broadway
Albany 12207

Main Post Office
115 Henry St.
Binghamton 13902

Bronx General Post Office
149th St. & Grand Concourse
Bronx 10401

U.S. Post Office
Parkchester Station
1449 West Avenue
Bronx 10462

U.S. Post Office
Riverdale Station
5951 Riverdale Ave.
Bronx 10471

U.S. Post Office
Throggs Neck Station
3630 East Tremont Ave.
Bronx 10465

U.S. Post Office
Wakefield Station
4165 White Plains Rd.
Bronx 10466

U.S. Post Office
Bay Ridge Station
5501 Seventh Ave.
Brooklyn 11229

Brooklyn General Post Office
271 Cadman Plaza East
Brooklyn 11201

U.S. Post Office
Greenpoint Station
66 Meserole Ave.
Brooklyn 11222

U.S. Post Office
Homecrest Station
2002 Avenue U
Brooklyn 11229

U.S. Post Office
Kensington Station
421 McDonald Avenue
Brooklyn 11218

Main Post Office
1200 William St.
Buffalo 14240

Main Post Office
1836 Mott Ave.
Far Rockaway 11691

Main Post Office
41-65 Main St.
Flushing 11351

U.S. Post Office
Ridgewood Station
869 Cypress Ave.
Flushing 11385

Main Post Office
Old Glenham Rd.
Glenham 12527

Main Post Office
16 Hudson Ave.
Glens Falls 12801

Main Post Office
185 West John St.
Hicksville 11802

Main Post Office
88-40 164th St.
Jamaica 11431

U.S. Post Office
Ansonia Station
1980 Broadway
New York 10023

U.S. Post Office
Bowling Green Station
25 Broadway
New York 10004

U.S. Post Office
Church Street Station
90 Church Street
New York 10007

U.S. Post Office
Empire State Station
350 Fifth Avenue
New York 10001

U.S. Post Office
F.D.R. Station
909 Third Ave.
New York 10022

U.S. Post Office
Grand Central Station
45th St. & Lexington Ave.
New York 10017

Madison Square Station
149 East 23rd St.
New York 10010

New York General Post Office
33rd & 8th Ave.
New York 10001

U.S. Post Office
Rockefeller Center Station
610 Fifth Avenue
New York 10020

U.S. Post Office
Times Square Station
340 West 42nd Street
New York 10036

Main Post Office
Franklin & S. Main
Pearl River 10965

Main Post Office
55 Mansion St.
Poughkeepsie 12601

Main Post Office
1335 Jefferson Rd.
Rochester 14692

Rockville Centre Main Post Office
250 Merrick Rd.
Rockville Centre 11570

Main Post Office
25 Route 111
Smithtown 11787

Main Post Office
550 Manor Road
Staten Island 10314

New Springville Station
2843 Richmond Ave.
Staten Island 10314

Main Post Office
5640 East Taft Rd.
Syracuse 13220

Main Post Office
10 Broad St.
Utica 13503

Main Post Office
143 Grand Street
White Plains 10602

NORTH CAROLINA
U.S. Post Office
Eastway Station
3065 Eastway Dr.
Charlotte 28205

U.S. Post Office
301 Green St.
Fayetteville 28302

U.S. Post Office
Fort Bragg Branch
Main Post Shopping Area
Riley Road
Fayetteville 28307

U.S. Post Office
310 New Bern Ave.
Raleigh 27611

NORTH DAKOTA
Main Post Office
657 Second Ave. N.
Fargo 58102

OHIO
Main Post Office
675 Wolf Ledges Parkway
Akron 44309

Main Post Office
2650 N. Cleveland Ave.
Canton 44701

U.S. Post Office
Fountain Square Station
5th and Walnut Sts.
Cincinnati 45202

Main Post Office
301 W. Prospect Ave.
Cleveland 44101

Main Post Office
850 Twin Rivers Drive
Columbus 43216

Main Post Office
1111 East Fifth St.
Dayton 45401

Main Post Office
200 N. Diamond St.
Mansfield 44901

Main Post Office
200 N. Fourth St.
Steubenville 43952

Main Post Office
435 S. St. Clair St.
Toledo 46301

Main Post Office
99 South Walnut St.
Youngstown 44503

OKLAHOMA

U.S. Post Office
101 East First
Edmond 73034

U.S. Post Office
115 West Broadway
Enid 73701

U.S. Post Office
102 South Fifth
Lawton 73501

525 West Okmulgee
Muskogee 74401

U.S. Post Office
129 West Gray
Norman 73069

U.S. Post Office
76320 SW 5th
Oklahoma City 73125

U.S. Post Office
333 West 4th
Tulsa 74101

U.S. Post Office
12 South Fifth
Yukon 73099

OREGON

Main Post Office
715 N.W. Hoyt
Portland 97208

PENNSYLVANIA

Main Post Office
442-456 Hamilton St.
Allentown 18101

U.S. Post Office
Lehigh Valley Branch
Airport Rd. & Route 22
Bethlehem 18001

Main Post Office
Beaver Drive Industrial Park
Du Bois 15801

Main Post Office
Griswold Plaza
Erie 16501

Main Post Office
238 S. Pennsylvania Ave.
Greensburg 15601

Main Post Office
10th & Market Sts.
Harrisburg 17105

Main Post Office
11 Franklin St.
Johnstown 15901

Main Post Office
1 W. Washington St.
Newcastle 16101

Main Post Office
30th & Market Sts.
Philadelphia 19104

U.S. Post Office
B. Free Franklin Station
316 Market St.
Philadelphia 19106

U.S. Post Office
William Penn Annex Station
9th & Chestnut Sts.
Philadelphia 19107

Main Post Office
Seventh Avenue & Grant St.
Pittsburgh 15219

Main Post Office
59 North 5th St.
Reading 19603

Main Post Office
North Washington Ave. &
Linden St.
Scranton 18503

Main Post Office
237 South Frazer St.
State College 16801

PUERTO RICO
San Juan General Post Office
Roosevelt Avenue
San Juan 00936

U.S. Post Office
Plaza Las Americas Station
San Juan 00938

RHODE ISLAND
Main Post Office
24 Corliss St.
Providence 02904

SOUTH CAROLINA
U.S. Post Office
85 Broad St.
Charleston 29401

U.S. Post Office
1601 Assembly St.
Columbia 29201

U.S. Post Office
600 W. Washington
Greenville 29602

SOUTH DAKOTA
(No philatelic outlets)

TENNESSEE
U.S. Post Office
9th & Georgia
Chattanooga 37401

U.S. Post Office
Tom Murray Station
133 Tucket St.
Jackson 38301

U.S. Post Office
501 W. Main Avenue
Knoxville 37901

U.S. Post Office
555 South Third
Memphis 38101

U.S. Post Office
Crosstown Finance Unit
1520 Union St.
Memphis 38104

U.S. Post Office
901 Broadway
Nashville 37202

TEXAS
U.S. Post Office
2300 South Ross
Amarillo 79105

U.S. Post Office
300 East South St.
Arlington 76010

U.S. Post Office
300 East Ninth
Austin 78710

U.S. Post Office
307 Willow St.
Beaumont 77704

U.S. Post Office
809 Neuces Bay
Corpus Christi 78408

U.S. Post Office
Bryan & Ervay Sts.
Dallas 75221

U.S. Post Office
5300 East Paisano Dr.
El Paso 79910

U.S. Post Office
Jennings & Lancaster Sts.
Fort Worth 76101

U.S. Post Office
408 Main St.
Hereford 79045

U.S. Post Office
401 Franklin Ave.
Houston 77001

U.S. Post Office
1515 Avenue "G"
Lubbock 79408

U.S. Post Office
100 East Wall
Midland 79702

U.S. Post Office
615 East Houston
San Antonio 78205

U.S. Post Office
2211 North Robinson
Texarkana 75501

U.S. Post Office
221 West Ferguson
Tyler 75702

U.S. Post Office
800 Franklin
Waco 76701

U.S. Post Office
1000 Lamar St.
Wichita Falls 76307

UTAH
Main Post Office
1760 West 2100 South
Salt Lake City 84119

VERMONT
Main Post Office
1 Elmwood Ave.
Burlington 05401

VIRGINIA
Main Post Office
1155 Seminole Trail
Charlottesville 22906

U.S. Post Office
Merrifield Branch
8409 Lee Highway
Fairfax 22031

Main Post Office
600 Granby St.
Norfolk 23501

U.S. Post Office
Thomas Corner Station
6274 East Virginia Beach Blvd.
Norfolk 23502

Main Post Office
1801 Brook Road
Richmond 23232

Main Post Office
419 Rutherford Ave. NE
Roanoke 24022

U.S. Post Office
London Bridge Station
550 First Colonial Rd.
Virginia Beach 23454

WASHINGTON
U.S. Post Office
Crossroads Station
15800 N.E. 8th
Bellevue 98008

Main Post Office
301 Union St.
Seattle 98101

Main Post Office
West 904 Riverside
Spokane 99210

Main Post Office
1102 A Street
Tacoma 98402

WEST VIRGINIA
Main Post Office
Lee and Dickinson Sts.
Charleston 25301

Main Post Office
217 King St.
Martinsburg 25401

WISCONSIN
Main Post Office
325 East Walnut
Green Bay 54301

Main Post Office
345 W. St. Paul Ave.
Milwaukee 53203

WYOMING
Main Post Office
2120 Capitol Ave.
Cheyenne 82001

Index